D1523405

A Century Is Not Enough

A Century Is
Not Enough

Sourav Ganguly
with
Gautam Bhattacharya

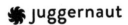 juggernaut

JUGGERNAUT BOOKS
KS House, 118 Shahpur Jat, New Delhi 110049, India

First published by Juggernaut Books 2018

Copyright © Sourav Ganguly 2018

10 9 8 7 6 5 4 3 2 1

The views and opinions expressed in this book are the author's own. The facts contained herein were reported to be true as on the date of publication by the author to the publishers of the book, and the publishers are not in any way liable for their accuracy or veracity.

All rights reserved. No part of this publication may be reproduced, transmitted, or stored in a retrieval system in any form or by any means without the written permission of the publisher.

ISBN 9789386228567

Typeset in Adobe Caslon Pro by R. Ajith Kumar, New Delhi

Printed at Manipal Technologies Limited

*To the memory of my father, my immediate family
and all the players I have played with*

*This book is also dedicated to Jagmohan Dalmiya
with respect and love. He is no longer with us but
I wish he could have read this book.*

Contents

Contents

Part 3: Giving Up Is Not an Option

Preface

Cricket was very important in my life, probably its most important aspect. By the grace of God, I could pursue what I wanted and make a career out of it. Playing this game for a long period gave me a life, financially and professionally. It gave me recognition, a place among the successful in society, and most important a tremendous amount of self-confidence. Cricket may be a sport to some, but to me it was life and very close to my heart.

During the course of my playing career it was not just the runs and wickets that were important – yes, they were – but I had to perform to play for that long. In my journey of success and failure, cricket taught me much about life, which I want to share with you in this book. From the outside most people see the adulation and hero worship but what does not get seen is the mind within. The tough periods, the important phases where you are just a little bit down . . . at times at painful crossroads . . . it happens to the best. At this stage it is important how you react. They say there is no backward step in life. For me there wasn't. And this was something sport taught me.

Preface

Sport poses many challenges along the way and it teaches you to take tough decisions in life, which is so important for longevity in sport. In this book I hope to show you the real challenge in sport. It is a fascinating challenge. A challenge which is worth taking. Always take the challenging path. You will end up the winner.

Part One

Climbing to the Top

1

Announcing the End

It was Durga Puja. As with all Bengalis, it's my favourite festival.

Our para Puja pandal is just a stone's throw from my house. Every year, I would not just visit it and offer my prayers but also play the occasional dhak, distribute prasad to the public and even do a bit of dhunuchi dancing during evening arati.

I knew that I was being watched as I celebrated. That there were people taking photos as I danced and played the drum. But I couldn't care less. During the Puja I was just like everyone else – the local para boy enjoying his favourite festival with all the glee of boyhood.

I am so hooked to the Pujas that I make it a point to always accompany the deity on her final ride. In Bengali there is a semi-tragic word for it – bisharjon. This is when the deity is immersed in the Ganga. The scene is amazing – the energy is sky-high, the crowds full of joy and sorrow at seeing Durga Ma going away, it's truly memorable. The area around the river is so crowded that once, during my Indian captaincy days, I decided to go disguised as one of Harbhajan's tribe. Yes, disguised as a sardarji.

Now I could have been mobbed big time. The situation could have gone out of control. But the thrill of accompanying the para boys and family members on the truck carrying the deity was just too irresistible.

My wife, Dona, had arranged for a make-up artist to come home to turn me from a hardcore Bengali into a convincing-looking Sikh. My cousins all mocked me, saying I would be recognized. I gave as good as I got and took up the challenge.

They turned out to be right. I was not allowed on the truck by the police and had to follow it in our car with my daughter, Sana. As the car reached the Babughat area the police inspector peered in through the window, looked closely at me and smiled gently in recognition. I was embarrassed but asked him to keep my secret. The escapade was worth it. The immersion scene around the river is just indescribable. You have to see it to understand it. Durga Ma after all comes only once a year.

Little did I know that the toughest decision of my life was to be announced on a Puja day in 2008. On Mahastami, when celebrations are usually at their peak, two days before the Bengaluru Test, I took part in a press conference. There I announced that I would retire from international cricket at the end of the series, after the last Test match in Nagpur. The bisharjon was still two days away but I had decided to bring an end to my cricketing career. It was 'The End' as they say in the movies. I was so emotionally drained that the Pujas that year passed me by in a blur. I don't remember a thing.

Almost a decade has gone by. Yet journalists and the Kolkata press still gossip about the events leading to my decision, and what I felt at the time. Surely I couldn't have felt as decisive and calm as I appeared that Mahastami day. Even this week as I write this, a close journalist friend asked me with a raised eyebrow, 'Come on, you don't expect me to believe that after so much trauma you did not cry after playing the last innings in Nagpur?'

I replied, no. I don't shed tears. I did not cry even at my father's death. Most of you, like my friend, won't believe me. Sourav is not telling the truth, you'll be saying to yourself. But some of you will be nodding your head in agreement. You know my type. We are a minority who tend to think tears are the easy way out of sadness. But don't let our masks fool you. Maybe it's because we hold our emotions in check that they remain within us even more. We look tough on the outside, but inside we bleed.

The events of that summer afternoon in 2008 still remain a raw wound for me. I was going for practice at Eden Gardens and had almost reached Fort William, which was just two minutes away. Suddenly my mobile rang. The caller happened to be a journalist. He had heard the news that I had been left out of the Rest of India squad, which is a clear indicator of how the selectors feel about you.

Me dropped? The Asian batsman and player of the year left out from a Rest of India team, I asked myself. After having scored consistently for the last three and a half years for India? But why? It can't have been my skill as I had only failed in one series in Sri Lanka where, apart from one batsman, none of my colleagues had done well. Yet they had all got picked.

I was angry. Disillusioned.

Hanging up, I told the driver to turn back and go home. I was in no mood to practise. This action made it clear to me that my chances of playing for India were now pretty low. My driver was unsure. He hesitantly looked at me, as if to get a final confirmation. My face must have said it all – he turned the car around quietly. I reached home and sat in front of the television, wondering to myself, so what's next?

People talk about the plusses of being a successful sportsman. The fame, the money and the high that it brings. Not many understand the tough side of the lives of sportsmen. Not only does age catch up with you but even after a glittering career you continue to be judged by others. This scrutiny decides your fate.

Never forget that through their career sportsmen often have only a single option for work. Rejection from national selectors or the cricket team closes all doors. Most of you can switch jobs. If you are not happy with the Ambanis, you can apply to the Tatas. If the Tatas reject you, you can try Infosys. The paths are many. For us cricketers, we have only one job. India placement. There is no other job. It is simple – India or nothing.

I have rarely missed a practice session. But that day I wanted to get away from all the hustle and bustle. I wanted a peaceful mind to chart out my future. I decided to call up the captain of my team and try to get to the bottom of the mess. Anil Kumble had been a friend and dear colleague for a long time.

I asked him point-blank, did he think I was no longer an automatic choice in his eleven? Kumble – the gentleman that he has always been – seemed embarrassed with my call.

He told me he hadn't been consulted before the selection committee chaired by Dilip Vengsarkar took this decision.

I believed him. I believed he had the courage to tell me honestly if he had been consulted. I had one more question for him. Did he still believe that his team wanted my services? I had been a captain for a long time and knew such a clarification was the best way forward.

Kumble's reply consoled me. He said if it came to him taking the call, he would pick me again for the upcoming Test match selection. I heaved a great sigh of relief. There was hope after all. I had two choices then. One, do nothing – sit back at home, watch TV and wait for the team selection. That would have been nerve-racking.

Choice number two. Go and play domestic cricket and convey a strong message to the selectors. Attitude is important. It is what separates the men from the boys. I was confident of my ability and knew if I was selected on the basis of my batting, no one could stop me. Around that time I could only think of one cricket tournament that was coming up, the JP Atrya Memorial Trophy in Chandigarh.

I called M.P. Pandove, the lifeblood of the Punjab Cricket Association, to tell him I desperately needed a team to play. He was of immense help and quietly obliged me even though my request had come in at the last minute.

I mean no disrespect to the tournament but most of you outside the northern cricketing belt have probably never heard of the JP Atrya Memorial Trophy. Even I knew of it only vaguely. But now things were different. In cricketing terminology the asking rate was climbing up and I urgently needed to respond. Look, no one has and no one will stay at the top forever. The more you condition your mind to the worst, the more you will feel ease at the top. I felt I needed to go and play. So I did. No ego. No negative thoughts. I just reacted to the situation.

It was the seven toughest days of my cricketing career. After having played in more than 400 international games, I had to play a tournament where I did not even know any of the players. Although I had scored more than 18,000 international runs, the runs I had to score here felt as urgent to me as in any international Test match. These runs were talking to me from the inside. Telling me, you are still good enough, still capable of scoring runs anywhere. Your love has not deserted you. The love for the game.

Alone in my Chandigarh hotel room, I thought to myself that this was truly surreal. Just three months ago at a glittering function in Karachi I was awarded a prize for being Asia's best batsman. Due to my commitments I couldn't make it to the ceremony. Dona had flown down to Karachi and accepted the award on my behalf. And here I was in this mess. It was like driving a Rolls-Royce one day and sleeping on the pavement the next.

I have had rejections, disappointments, tragedies all my cricketing life. I have been at the receiving end of truly vicious gossip. I have lost count of how often I have come back from the jaws of getting rejected. At times I felt my life resembled a roller coaster. As they say in Hindi, kabhi upar, kabhi nichey. It could have broken the spine of someone who was talented but emotionally weak. But I have always been a fighter. I have handled the bad news head-on, and embraced pressure as part of the package.

I told myself that this too was an investment. My experience had taught me that I played best when I worked the hardest. So I continued to believe that my time would come. I knew I was a winner. Being a winner is about what happens in your head. And I had never lost the belief in myself. I looked at a cricket ground and believed it was mine. Looked at the pitch and believed we would win. Looked at the bat and told myself I would score runs. I woke up every morning to succeed.

The Indian team for the first two Test matches of the Australian series was soon announced. I found my name in it. Simultaneously a Board President's team was also announced. This was the secondary team that would take on the Australians in Chennai. The Board President's XI is traditionally used to vet the potential of promising youngsters or assess veterans whose Test future is uncertain.

I was included in it as well. These teams got picked by the new selection committee under Krishnamachari Srikkanth. But its mindset seemed to be no different from the previous committee's. The message was crystal clear – that a veteran of 100-plus Test matches, a certain Sourav Ganguly, was again on trial.

I felt extremely agitated. That is when I told my father that I needed to call it a day. Enough was enough. My father was a bit surprised. In the past when Greg Chappell had kept me out of the team and I was desperately fighting to claw my way back, he had wanted me to retire, unable to bear his son's struggle.

Then I had resisted. I had told him, Bapi, you wait. I will be back. I still have cricket left in me. When I grow older I don't want to sit on my sofa and tell myself, Sourav, you gave up when the going was tough. You should have tried harder. I wanted to catch the bull by its horns and win.

So three years later when he heard the same person was throwing in the towel, he was surprised. I also told my wife and my mother but no one else. None of my friends had a clue. The story didn't leak. Not even in the Kolkata media, which I was often accused of favouring.

I of course had a chat with Anil before I reached Chennai. He told me, don't decide anything in a hurry. Give it some time. I assured him I would. But deep down I knew my time was up. I made up my mind that I would give everything I had to be successful in this series.

But I wouldn't let anyone else decide my future any more. I wouldn't go through the ordeal again. I had had enough! Yes, I was angry. After reaching Bengaluru I informed Kumble that my mind was made up and I would announce shortly.

Cricketing history has recorded that I had an outstanding final series. Got a hundred in Mohali and narrowly missed the second in Nagpur. I was surprised at how good I was feeling. I saw the same attitude in Sachin when he played his last Test match in Wankhede. His innings was one of the best I had seen him play towards the later stages of his career. I felt that no one could do me any harm any more. I could fly freely.

In Mohali a journalist came and asked, 'Did the hundred give you special pleasure because Greg Chappell was watching it from the Australian camp?' I said, at this stage of my cricketing career it didn't matter at all. I had got past all that. For me he didn't exist any more.

I still remember the walk out to the pitch in my last Test. As I went out to bat, the Australian team under Ricky Ponting gave me a guard of honour as a sign of respect. It was very moving, and I felt very honoured by their gesture. But I knew, irrespective of the respect shown, the moment Brett Lee went back to his bowling mark, his first delivery would be aimed at my nose.

That is always the reality in top-class sport. In the end all that matters is to win. The man the Indian selectors had kept on an indefinite trial did stand up to the Australian attack and walked away with a solid 85. I missed the coveted three-figure mark only by 15 runs but my friend Sach lent an additional flavour to the party by getting a rock-solid hundred. What made the occasion happier was that we won the Test.

I ended my final innings in Test cricket in a first-ball duck. Looking back I still feel it was a loose shot as I tried to play Jason Krejza against the turn. The bat had closed early and Krejza easily accepted a low return catch. I have no regrets. It was a bad shot and I paid the price. But I still regret missing the hundred. It was mine for the taking.

As the match came to a close, Mahendra Singh Dhoni in a surprise gesture asked me to lead. I had rejected his offer earlier in the day, but could not refuse a second time. Ironically, my captaincy career had begun exactly eight years ago on this very day. I handled the bowling changes and field placements while the last Australian wicket batted.

But I must admit, at that stage, I found it difficult to focus. So after three overs I handed it back to Dhoni saying, it is your job, MS. We both smiled.

I was filled with mixed emotions. I felt extremely sad that the biggest love of my life was going away. On the other hand, I felt deeply satisfied that I had held my head high right till the end. I had competed with the best cricket team in the world in my final series and performed admirably. It proved that a certain Sourav Ganguly was still good enough.

Anil had retired a week before at the Kotla. The Vidarbha Cricket Association had organized a joint farewell reception for both of us. The entire board was present to hand over mementos to us. I asked Anil, are you ready to finish? He said he was.

His answer consoled me. I felt if the captain of the team didn't want to continue, my decision was right. Notwithstanding selectorial whims and fancies, I could not see anyone taking our places in the side. Yet he thought this was the right time to go.

Once the felicitations finished, the party began. Members of the team had organized a night for us at the hotel. All of us really let our hair down. Some of us even went berserk. I have been around in Indian cricket for more than fifteen years and I have never experienced anything as warm, as wild and as fun as this party was.

It was a night neither Anil nor I will forget. One's fellow cricketers' admiration counts a lot for a pro, however big he may be. I received a shirt from my teammates which was signed by all of them. It said, we will miss you. I was truly moved.

And so it was all over. From 11 November 2008 Sourav Ganguly was a retired Test cricketer. I was also not part of the one-day team.

I always knew that this day would arrive and I was extremely happy at what I had achieved. It was time to march on. Think of the magical moments I had experienced along the way and remind myself that it had been an extraordinary run. There really was nothing more I could have asked from life.

2

Wilderness at Down Under

The world's scariest fast bowler was staring intensely at me from across the pitch with a ball in his hand. The cricketing world bowed down before him. He was viewed as a universal dangerman. He was Mr Malcolm Marshall, one of the quartet of West Indian fast bowlers who dominated the game in the late 1980s and early 1990s – Marshall, Ambrose, Patterson and Walsh.

They say you return to your childhood increasingly as you turn old. I began to visit my cricketing childhood as I hung up my bat from Test cricket. At the Nagpur stadium, as I was giving away some of my cricketing shirts and gear to my fans, the scene from the Gabba flashed in front of my eyes.

What a way to begin one's international career! It was 11 January 1992. We were playing West Indies in a triangular series in Brisbane. Now the Gabba has always been a fast bowler's paradise. Marshall on that surface was easily more menacing than his usual self. To make matters worse, my preparation had consisted of two months of almost no net practice and some infrequent throwdowns. I have since tried to erase the memory of that match as much as possible. It was a huge learning curve.

For me, it was a journey literally from the coal mines to the Indian dressing room. I was only nineteen years old and playing in one of the local tournaments in Jamadoba, Jharkhand, when I got a call from the Indian selector Rusi Jeejeebhoy. He told me that I stood a good chance of getting into the Indian team.

Now Rusi was the coach of our Under 15 and Under 19 Indian teams – where I had already made my mark as a match-winning batsman. He had closely followed my development as a cricketer and had witnessed my century against an Under 19 Pakistan in Mumbai. A great believer in me, he had forcefully argued for me at the selection committee meeting.

Rusi had his way. I got included in the squad of seventeen for the three-match one-day series against South Africa in India and also for the Australian tour that followed. I was simply over the moon. Please remember, I was not even twenty!

The series attracted huge attention worldwide. It marked the return of South Africa to world cricket after years and years of isolation because of their apartheid policy. The atmosphere in Eden Gardens was electrifying during the opening match. More than one lakh people had turned up. It was history in the making and I remained a wide-eyed teenager right in the middle of it, trying to take in everything that was happening around me.

The team was announced a day earlier and I was in the reserves. With a strong middle order consisting of Azhar, Tendulkar, Manjrekar and Amre, it was difficult to find a place for myself in the playing eleven. My first roommate in the Indian team was Pravin Amre, who played an active role in the opening match.

I was fine not playing. For me, being at Eden Gardens with the Indian team was good enough. As a reserve player I accompanied the drinks trolley and ran in with gloves whenever someone needed them. I was so happy doing the chores that the rest didn't matter. I had grown up watching Kapil Dev, Azhar, Vengsarkar, and played with Tendulkar from a very young age. To be part of that elite group, that too playing at Eden Gardens where I had spent my childhood, was a dream come true.

To be honest I used to have an inferiority complex sitting in the dressing room alongside these greats. I would look at Vengsarkar, 'the colonel', and think I have seen this man score a hundred against the likes of Patterson and Davies. This man has scored three centuries at Lord's and now I am sitting next to him. How can this be true?

Then there was Kapil Dev. I was flying kites on the very afternoon he had scored that immortal 175 at Tunbridge Wells. I also remembered him standing tall at the Lord's balcony and holding the World Cup. What a sight it was!

Azharuddin, our captain, was another attraction. I saw him score a hundred in his debut Test match at the Eden. I felt just like a school kid whose parents have brought him to meet his heroes. If anyone had asked me what was discussed at the team meetings, I would have been embarrassed. I spent all my time observing the legends and barely paid attention to the conversations.

Soon it was time to depart for the Australia tour. My parents had come down to Delhi to see me off. You have to understand that I come from a conservative, close-knit family and so my parents were with me at our hotel to say goodbye.

The players were making their way to the elevators one by one. My mother looked at Sachin with wide eyes and said below her breath, oh, he is so small. Sachin in those days used to sport the Saibaba kind of hairstyle and he had already become the hero of the nation. In another three months' time he would be described by the media as the kiss of life for Test cricket.

There was a fellow Bengali in the team. Another player from East Zone. Subrata Banerjee. Subu, as he was affectionately called, was not just an exceptional bowler but a genuine all-rounder. The cricket manager of the team was a former opener of India, Abbas Ali Baig.

In those days, before the arrival of Ajit Wadekar, the role of the Indian cricket manager was not very important. Abbas was one of those blue-blooded gentleman but he hardly spoke. He also represented the old school of cricket and may not have been in tune with the modern game that was changing rapidly.

We flew Air India in economy class. In those days Indian cricketers could not think of flying business class as the Board of Cricket Control in India (BCCI) wasn't rich. We landed at Perth and checked into the Sheraton. Unless you were the captain or the seniormost player, single rooms were out of the question. You had to double up with a team member. I was given a roommate. Mr Dilip Vengsarkar.

I had only played a few first-class matches and here was a former Indian captain who had played 100-plus Test matches. I was so much in awe of Vengsarkar that I could barely open my mouth in front of him. I just did what he did and made sure that I didn't do anything to annoy or distract the great man. In fact I was so shy of him that I stayed away from the room as much as possible.

Vengsarkar's best friend was Chandrakant Pandit, the second wicketkeeper. They mostly spent time together and talked in Marathi. I found shelter instead in Sachin's room. His roommate was Subu. We would chat non-stop in Bengali even with Sachin in the room.

I had played with Sachin at the Under 15 level and we were almost the same age so I felt very comfortable with him. Vengsarkar meanwhile got curious as I never seemed to be in our room. He asked me one day, 'Where do you go in the evening?' I couldn't tell him the truth – that I was too self-conscious to be alone with him.

On the first day of the tour I was sitting alone in the hotel lounge downstairs. I was a bit jet-lagged. Suddenly one of the lifts opened and a legendary Indian cricketer came out. He asked me what I was doing for dinner. I had made plans but didn't dare say that. So we went out.

As we walked through the streets of Perth, half of the restaurants had already shut. With some difficulty we managed to find a Chinese joint. Whenever I am in Perth I still go to that place and remember the conversation we had that day. I did not have the guts to ask him questions or argue back and was only a patient listener.

The only question I managed to ask was how he thought the tour would play out. He said Australia was a very difficult place to play cricket in and that as a young player

I should never have made the trip. He mentioned another young player's name from Delhi who he felt should have made this tour and indicated that I didn't deserve to be here.

His words really shook me. Was he telling me indirectly that I did not deserve a place in the side? The cricketer's unkind words left a deep emotional scar. Perhaps it was not said to undermine my confidence. He might have sincerely been trying to prepare me for the challenges of playing in Australia. But it was hardly the way to motivate a shy and nervous youngster who was trying to find his feet in international cricket.

Our traditional tour opener against the ACB Chairman's XI was at the iconic WACA. My colleagues warned me about the additional pace and bounce of the ground. I saw it for myself as soon as I entered the practice arena. It was a completely different kind of track. I did play in Perth after that. But the wickets in 1991–92 were much quicker and harder.

The Indian team's training and fitness methods were completely different from what they are today. If what I saw when I started off in 1991 was North Pole then when I finished in 2008 it was South Pole. It seemed only two cricketers from the team felt the need to train – Kapil Dev and Javagal Srinath. As frontline pace bowlers they had to remain fit. Manoj Prabhakar also did a fair bit of physical exercises. The rest of the unit including some of our star batsmen simply did not believe in it.

Our first game in Perth was a day-nighter. But the competition was so one-sided that the match was over before the lights were switched on at the WACA. Bruce Reid and

Mike Whitney broke the back of Indian batting and hinted at the shape of things to come.

This Indian team had played their last match only a couple of days ago in Delhi – the third and last one-dayer against South Africa. But the difference between the surface in that match and the one here was enormous.

Even then I could see that scoring runs in those Australian conditions required completely different batting skills, and the batting unit had to get used to horizontal bat shots. As the days went by and our batsmen kept on failing both in the Tests and in the one-dayers, the gloom in our dressing room intensified. Our morale was at an all-time low.

Our struggling Indian batsmen, some of whom looked woefully out of form, simply couldn't adjust to the tough conditions in Australia – the quality of attack was just too brilliant. Mind you, we had in our ranks some of the classiest players who had done exceedingly well in the West Indies or England against some express fast bowling. But batting in South Africa and Australia is a different ball game altogether. The bounce is different. The pace is different. In England you could come on to the front foot and recover. Even in the West Indies. Not here.

By the time Ravi Shastri scored a double century in Sydney and Sachin an absolute masterclass innings of 114 in Perth, the series was over. Azhar also got a dazzling hundred in Adelaide but India ended up losing that Test match as well. The Brisbane and Melbourne Tests finished in three days. Forget full five days of Test cricket, we were not even competing on the fourth day.

Sitting outside, I could clearly see that the Indian batting could not cope with the additional bounce and pace, especially the bounce. Our batsmen played with much lower wrists than what was needed to combat such an attack.

By the time they adjusted to the Aussie wickets, the carnage was over. McDermott, Merv Hughes, Whitney and Reid literally finished them. Reid with his 6'7" frame was the toughest to handle as he bounced deliveries from a good length. The rest of the bowlers were not so unplayable but even they did not allow the Indian batsmen to come on to the front foot.

Sanjay Manjrekar, in particular, must have felt very disappointed. He had come to this tour with a huge reputation, having scored against some fearsome attacks in Pakistan and in the West Indies. But by the end of the series, his reputation and confidence had taken a severe beating. As the defeats piled up, Sanjay, a perfectionist, had worry written all over his face. He also seemed frustrated with his failure.

One day after a side game, he called me to his room and gave me a lashing. He told me that I was not behaving properly and that my attitude needed to improve, now that I was an international cricketer. I was completely taken aback and did not respond. After fifteen minutes in his room, I left silently with a dark cloud hanging over my head. What was he talking about? And why?

Two months had gone by in this tour and I was struggling to get even a proper hit at the nets. From a batsman I had been reduced to a net bowler helping our batsmen practise.

So where had I gone wrong? Today Sanjay is a good friend and a loving fellow commentator but to this day I have not understood why he behaved so differently with a youngster on his first tour. I certainly did not deserve this dressing-down.

In Sydney, India fared much better. But that's because we got lucky. Reid, the chief tormentor of India, left the field after the first hour with a side sprain. He didn't return for the rest of the series. The Sydney Test will also remain significant for a different reason. It saw the debut of Shane Warne. He was chubbier then and got hit all over the park by Shastri and Sachin. This was Sachin's first hundred in Australia.

Another person making his debut was Subrata Banerjee. Subu had bowled very well at the Sydney Cricket Ground (SCG) to capture three wickets in the first innings. But in the second he was not used even for a single over by captain Azhar. This decision had raised eyebrows and was discussed for years to come.

I felt Subu was not used because of Azhar's over-reliance on the other pacers. India had put pressure on Australia for the first time in that series and Azhar went back to his tried-and-tested trio of bowlers – Kapil, Prabhakar and Srinath.

Shastri was the lone spinner but by then he was focusing more on his batting. He had sent down 25 overs to pick three wickets, which was decent, but we needed firepower from the other end. Even Tendulkar was used as a bowler. But strangely not Subrata. In those days Indian captains had this tendency to use spinners excessively even outside the subcontinent. In retrospect I felt if Azhar had given the new ball to Subrata we may have won that Test which eventually ended in a draw.

Throughout the tour only two from our team did justice to their reputation. Kapil and Sachin. Kapil paaji bowled with fire and imagination to reach a landmark 400 Test wickets. A feat that had eluded Indian bowlers. Equally impressive was Sachin. He was easily the best batsman in the two teams.

I was particularly surprised to see the great Vengsarkar failing. By then my roommate had started to get on the wrong side of the game and was slow against genuine pace. After his failure in the first two Tests Vengsarkar's self-confidence was also dented. Despite getting two fifties in the series, he announced his retirement as soon as we returned.

Cricket lovers and journalists have asked me, what would have happened if my 2003 team to Australia had toured in 1991–92? Would they have surrendered so meekly? Two different generations can never be compared. The eras were different. The mindsets were different.

The reason I believed my frontline batsmen were much superior in those conditions was that India's visits to Australia had become more frequent. Players were more aware of the quality of pitches and adjusted their games to the conditions a lot quicker.

We had a Sehwag who attacked Australia in Australia. There was an impregnable Dravid at number 3 from where he anchored the team. The ever brilliant Laxman was at number 6. All brilliant players of fast bowling in all conditions. And of course Sachin, who was a much more complete batsman in 2003.

I am not suggesting that Azhar's batting line-up was

weak. On the contrary, the 1992 lower middle order was better with Kapil at 7, Prabhakar at 8 and Kiran More at 9. It must also be acknowledged that if the Australian attack that we handled from 1996 to 2004 was the best I have ever played, then the 1992 attack would be the second on the list.

I have played the two great Ws from Pakistan in their prime. I have played Ambrose and Walsh in the West Indies. Donald and Kallis in South Africa. In the 2002 England series as captain my batting line-up had to negotiate a combination of Flintoff–Harmison–Jones–Hoggard. They were outstanding – having raw pace as well as reverse swing. But the Australian attack comprising McDermott, Reid, Whitney and Hughes in my debut international series was simply top class.

There were stories that Ranbir Singh Mahendra, the administrative manager, wrote to me asking why I didn't carry drinks on to the field. That I had behaved arrogantly. It was also reported that I wrote to him complaining that I was getting ragged by the seniors. These stories are completely untrue. I kept hearing them again and again over the years. But I have no idea where they originated from.

There was, however, an incident involving me carrying the drinks on to the ground a bit late. This was at the SCG. I was at the old Sydney dressing room, where I had turned on the TV to listen to the iconic Channel Nine commentators Richie Benaud and Bill Lawry. I had a huge fascination for both. While Benaud was the soft-spoken, highly credible professor, Lawry was like a theatre jockey who kept the crowd on the edge of their seats.

The Indian team was out on the field but I remained

glued to the TV, sitting by myself in the dressing room. Throughout the series Kapil Dev was managing to get the better of Allan Border with his huge inswingers. Every time the ball would create a big gap between the bat and the pad and ensure Border's dismissal. Border bowled by Kapil was almost becoming a regular feature.

I was busy watching the replay of one such dismissal when a stern-looking Abbas Ali Baig marched in, ordering me to carry drinks on to the field. The moment a wicket falls, drinks or any other equipment that are needed are carried on to the field by the reserves. I was so engrossed in the TV commentary that I did not even realize that I was not watching a replay of the previous Test but a live coverage. Kapil paaji was that good on the tour even though his knees had almost given up.

As for me, I mostly watched and attempted to learn from the sidelines, barely managing to get a game in. I was picked on that tour as a batsman who could bowl a bit. However, in the first month of the tour I was reduced to being a bowler who could bat a bit.

Since I was not being considered a batter, it was impossible to get proper practice at the nets. It was frustrating, but the batsmen who were playing needed more time at the nets as the Aussie bowling was so tough.

I was a reserve batsman hoping to find a window somewhere. But who would bowl at me? Who would give me practice? So during the later stages of the tour, I carried my bowling boots rather than a bat in my kitbag. After all, what was the point.

I eventually got a chance to play against Queensland and

thought I batted pretty well in that match, especially against the seasoned Carl Rackemann.

Australia was pressing so hard that even for a side game like New South Wales versus India they fielded the strongest possible team, armed with the likes of Mark Taylor and the Waugh brothers. They would not give India even the slightest chance of coming back in the series. With the gloom surrounding our camp, my individual fortune also looked gloomy.

The Test matches were getting completely one-sided but we hoped for a better outcome in the triangular World Series Cup, where the West Indies, without the sensational Viv Richards, were the third team. This was the first time that I saw the West Indian players from up close. Ambrose, Richardson, Marshall, Walsh and the Prince, Brian Lara. One day both the teams were practising at the Adelaide Oval around the same time. They had arrived a little late and when we finished our practice they were still at the nets.

I had just caught hold of a few local net bowlers to give me some useful batting practice which had been denied me so far. Since our team bus was leaving I requested the manager to allow me a few extra minutes. He spoke to the West Indian manager and asked if I could be dropped back to the hotel by their team bus since we were at the same hotel. It was an unusual request but he readily said yes.

I will always remember that ride. As I got into the bus I spotted only one vacant seat in the front next to the great Curtly Ambrose. He was a giant of a man – his head was almost touching the baggage shelf of the bus and he had long, enormous hands. But contrary to his fearsome image on the field, I found him extremely jovial.

He was a typical West Indian who loved his music and guitar. He started singing the moment the bus began to move. When he sang, I noticed his lips almost touched his ears. The players were all singing, joking, dancing in the bus. The word 'pressure' or 'tension' did not seem to exist in their dictionary. The ambience in the Indian team bus on that tour, on the other hand, was very, very serious.

When I got a sudden nod to play against the West Indies that fateful day in January I found myself thoroughly underprepared. I had not picked the bat properly in two months! I quickly ran into the dressing room, caught hold of Venkatapathy Raju and begged him to give me some throwdowns. But that was hardly enough.

The captain had said I would go three down. To make my plight sadder the first three wickets went down early. The fiery West Indian fast bowlers had sorted our frontline batting pretty quickly.

I walked in and Marshall greeted the debutant in international cricket with a delivery that hit my pad. It was an incoming delivery and I had completely missed the line. I was extremely lucky not to be given out. There was a huge appeal which got dismissed.

Even today, I remain thankful to the umpire for his kindness even though I could not use it to my advantage. My luck did not last long. Very soon I was declared LBW to Anderson Cummins for just 3. Only Sachin stood out to score a fighting 77. But even his brilliance could not stop our six-wicket defeat. I was not asked to send down a single over and with just one batting failure it was curtains down on my tour appearances.

Little did I know that the India counter would only open for me after four long years of waiting. To be honest I felt as a player on that trip I was below the required level. It's not easy in Australia if you don't play regularly and I never settled down on that trip, nor was I given any opportunities to practise or any attention and advice. But the experience of that visit made me come back as a better player.

After Australia, India went back to their tried and trusted and I was ignored for the World Cup. The team was shortened to 14. Vengsarkar, Hirwani, Pandit and I were on our way back home. As I boarded the flight for India, all kinds of emotions coursed through my mind.

Some of it was sadness – I had spent three long months in a country barely playing. I wondered if I would get such an opportunity again. But I also realized that I needed to get stronger mentally. I had to improve my game to face top-quality fast bowling successfully. The tour had taught me what I required to do to succeed against the toughest.

It also highlighted a stark reality that in domestic cricket you may get two to three bad balls out of six which you can take advantage of. In Test cricket you may not get that one ball and have to learn instead to score consistently against good balls. Confidence and ability were the key. It's a difficult combination. You don't get to buy them in a supermarket.

I wanted to use all my experience gained in Australia to emerge as a better player. My journey may not have been successful but then failure has always been the best teacher! It taught me a lot and I came back stronger.

3

Maharaj, You Are In

I remember the evening as if it were yesterday. I was sitting on the steps of the upper tier of the Eden Gardens Club House and watching Azhar's India crumble against Sri Lanka. It was 1996, the World Cup semi-final. As a spectator, I had never witnessed anything as nerve-racking as this.

The crowd was getting extremely agitated with the fall of every Indian wicket. The emotions in the stadium were crazily high. With India's defeat imminent, a part of the crowd started throwing bottles into the stadium, and finally chairs were burnt in anger to the right of where I was sitting, on the CAB Annual Members' Stand.

The situation was completely out of hand. Match referee Clive Lloyd called off the game and declared Sri Lanka the winners. Kambli, helmet in his hand, walked off the ground with tears in his eyes, a scene that was captured on television all over the cricketing world.

I felt India had completely messed it up at the toss. Later, after I became captain, I realized that the decisions made on the cricket field by a captain are far more difficult than what a spectator like me judging it from an upper tier seat could ever imagine.

I must confess while the patriotic part of me wanted India to win at any cost, the cricketer part was thinking otherwise. India's unexpected defeat meant that someone like me who had done well in the domestic season stood a realistic chance of making it to the team. The team for Singapore and Sharjah was to be announced a few days later. To be honest if the team had won at Kolkata and made it to the finals at Lahore I would not have fancied my chances.

Finally the all-important day came. I was driving back home after a practice session at my club. In those days I had an old Maruti 800 which my grandfather had gifted me when I passed out of college.

In Bengal at the time, facilities were fairly rudimentary. You had to rely upon the club to provide you with the practice facilities once the state games got over. It was one of those typical practice afternoons. Except on this day I was impatient and edgy throughout the session. My mind was constantly wandering to the selection committee meeting in Mumbai.

I knew I had a good chance to wear the Indian cap again after four long years in the wilderness. My mind had already begun to leap ahead, just stopping short of imagining being on the field, with millions watching me on television. A cold shiver went down my spine every time I thought about the meeting in Mumbai. I knew that I was so close to achieving my dreams and yet there was no guarantee that it would happen.

I don't know how to describe the feelings I experienced

that afternoon. Most of you will have had a similar experience at least once in your lives – when you know you are facing a crucial moment in your life, a break that could change everything. It is restlessness, nervousness, anxiety all rolled into one as you await the curtains to open, the red carpet to roll out.

The waiting was soon over. A journalist friend gave me the news – I had missed the bus again. There was complete silence in the car. I don't think the driver and I even exchanged one word throughout the twenty-minute drive. Only one thought was going through my head – will I ever get another opportunity? It was a horrible, sinking feeling.

In such a hopeless situation you will have your parents, who are fellow travellers on your journey. They will try to console you. Their love and affection will remain regardless. But beyond a point it won't help you to get up and fight again.

It is your inner voice that has to eventually prompt you to set the desperation aside and pull you up. You have to tell yourself that the sun will rise tomorrow, you will have another opportunity. Yes, you will struggle with deep disappointment, endless frustration. But one day those feelings will come back to help you, pushing you to get to the next level.

To get over this, stand in front of the mirror and tell yourself, yes, I did lose yesterday, but my time will come. If you are a budding cricketer pack your equipment and make sure you get back to the place that provides the platform for recovery. That is, the cricket ground.

Always remember, if you decide to allow your frustrations

to rule, the next day will be even tougher. The world will move at its own pace and barely cares about your sentiments. I know it is easier said than done, but you will have to find a way to conquer the feeling of despondency.

As I sit down to write this, I must admit I did exactly the opposite. When I went to bed, I told myself that I was going to give training a miss the next day. The feeling of rejection was just a bit too painful to swallow. The morning after is especially bad.

India meanwhile went to play the tri-series. An apprehensive Sourav Ganguly once again sat in front of the TV trying to imagine how he would have performed in those match situations. The series finished soon and once again India fared badly. Well, hope raised its head again. The England tour was next and I knew that there would be another opportunity to get selected.

I was like a young boy desperately in love with a beautiful girl in college. You go to college every day wanting her to arrive quickly. Some days she will be late. And on certain days the mother, much to your disappointment, will whisk her away to some unknown destination. You will get angry. You will feel hopeless. You will feel low. But by the next morning, your patience will have renewed itself and you will be waiting at the college gate again.

Here I have a suggestion for any youngster wanting to achieve big. The cycle of hope and despair can crush you. It will destroy your confidence temporarily. But you have to look at it positively. Look at it as an integral part of your journey to excellence. Trust me, not many people even get an opportunity to be part of this cycle. It is not a bad position to be in. As for me I was constantly trying to tell myself to be positive, that my turn would come sooner or later.

It was the day of the England tour selection and I was once again at the maidan. This time I was at Eden Gardens to play East Bengal in an important local cricket match. I got a hundred that day. Around four in the afternoon a journalist friend walked up to me to say that the team would be announced any minute. This friend today works with me in my office and I still distinctly remember his reassuring second sentence. 'Tui dhukchis, Maharaj. You are in,' he said excitedly. Apparently he had been tipped off by a selector.

My expectation level was already high. Now it went up even further. I was trying to stay calm but how do you stay calm in such situations? I could hear my heart thumping. I could hardly stay still. It was an hour before the team was announced – and my name did figure in the list. I was so overwhelmed. I didn't know how to react. I just kept smiling, not knowing what to do.

Should I call my father? Or my mother? Or just sit idle on the lawns of Eden Gardens? It was one of the best feelings of my life. Fellow players came up and congratulated me. I went up and met Mr Jagmohan Dalmiya, an absolute father figure to me. I would not have reached so far without his unconditional support from a young age. He was very close to my father as well.

I returned home in the same Maruti 800, this time in a completely different frame of mind. I had waited for four long, painful years and my joy knew no bounds.

When I reached home my mother immediately took me

to the family prayer room. I come from a deeply religious family and my mother made sure that I thanked the Almighty first. I spent the day going through the motions of accepting congratulations, talking to family members and friends, but in my mind I was already boarding the flight to England, which was about a week away.

I also took the time to thank a few people immediately. Firstly, a gentleman called Arun Lal. I was always impressed with his personality and thinking and the way he motivated youngsters. Arun had made it openly known that I was ready to play for the country and spoken enthusiastically about me to a few Indian seniors he was close to.

Remember, we are talking about an India twenty-two years ago. There was no live telecast for Ranji matches. No ESPN CricInfo. No YouTube. Hearing was believing. Even before Sachin became Sachin, the Mumbai cricketers had started discussing him with players from other parts of the country. This is hugely helpful to a newcomer and Arun did that for me.

I was also very grateful to Sambaran Banerjee, the selector from my zone. To make it to the team, the selector has to be solidly behind you. In Sambaran I was fortunate to have someone who fought for me and tried hard to make the other zonal selectors believe in my capability. A selector or a captain can't bat for you. But they can create an atmosphere that will help you to perform. In that respect Sambaran was of great help.

I landed at Heathrow a week later carrying with me the extra baggage of being marked as someone who didn't deserve his place. There had been controversy surrrounding my selection. But luckily the media wasn't half as powerful then as it is now. Today, there wouldn't have been an escape. I would have been affected by all the negative news floating in. But with the quick departure to the United Kingdom I was mostly away from it all.

I had been in and around London several times playing league cricket. My father made sure that every summer I went to England to further my cricketing education. But he was strict and I didn't get a pound in hand. My respectable coach Debu Mitra, who I had looked up to since I was young, was completely in charge and paid everything for me. I also had some family there who had become my immediate family of sorts.

My kaka Animesh Mukherjee was my guardian in England and remains so till date. We share an amazing bond. My daughter Sana considers him and kakima as her grandparents. They were my second home, a relationship beyond words, there was so much care, love and affection. As a player I had huge success in England. It was as if my kaka was batting with me and my success suffused them with pride and joy.

I still vividly remember the drive from Heathrow to our Central London hotel. We were staying in a small hotel on Jermyn Street near Piccadilly. Sitting today in Kolkata I can tell you the exact location of the hotel – which turn to make from Piccadilly, exactly where the hotel was located in the narrow street. I still remember what the coffee shop looked like. What the colour of the ceiling of the hotel lobby was.

Whenever I go to London I make it a point to walk past this hotel. I stand near its front gate and waves of nostalgia wash over me. I once took my daughter to the hotel. As we walked inside the front gate, hand in hand, she looked up to see me break into a big smile.

Sana was a little surprised. By then she had already stayed in some of the best hotels in Central London and could not understand what the fuss about this one was. She had grown up seeing a successful dad and also heard a few stories about his cricketing exploits. 'Baba, what is the big deal about this place?' she asked. I smiled and said, Sanu, it all started from here.

As I mentioned earlier, the hotel was not a plush five-star. The rooms were pretty small; the breakfast spread wasn't spectacular. But despite all this, I have a deep sense of attachment with this simple little place. How can you lose touch with your origins?

I guess every time I visit this place, there is some unmistakable glow on my face. She must have noticed it. Her next question was, 'Baba, do you love the sport more? Or me?'

I looked at her and grinned.

4

The Haynes Discourse

How could I have known that everything would change at breakfast!

With the series hanging 1-0 in England's favour, the Indian team arrived in Manchester to play the last one-dayer. I remember the Manchester hotel distinctly as well. It was in the heart of the city and to me remains as memorable as Cavendish Hotel on Jermyn Street.

The drive from Heathrow to Manchester had been very refreshing. The minute we had hit the motorway with its many exits and seen the countryside outside our bus window, I had felt at peace. This was altogether a different world, completely away from the hustle and bustle of city life.

Ours was a day game which would begin at eleven. I was certain I wouldn't be in the eleven and walked into the breakfast lounge at a leisurely pace around half past eight, ready to enjoy a hearty English breakfast. I had sausages, bacon, sandwiches, some juice and went to the counter for a second helping.

That is when I bumped into our captain. Azhar had been looking for me. He told me, without any fanfare, 'You will play today and bat at number 3.' Before I could digest this I saw Rahul Dravid walking into the breakfast lounge.

We knew each other pretty well. Although he was a year junior, we had played Under 19 cricket together. He and I were also part of Kailash Gattani's team that had toured England earlier.

I of course vividly remembered Dravid's debut hundred in Ranji Trophy, which incidentally was scored against us at Eden Gardens. We had won that match thanks to my elder brother Snehasish's sensational innings. Despite being on the losing side, Rahul's hundred was discussed for years to come.

As he settled down to sit at the table just next to me, I quietly told him that I was batting at number 3 today. He asked, 'Who is missing out then?' I had no idea. I wasn't brave enough to ask the captain of India, though I felt it had to be Sidhu.

Dravid got up to get some juice. I saw Azhar walking up and talking to him. So he could be playing as well. He came back and confirmed it. I asked what number. Dravid shook his head and said he didn't know.

My gut, I told him, was that he would bat at number 6. Tendulkar would open with Vikram Rathore. Manjrekar would come at 4 and Azhar at 5. The conversation ended right there. So did breakfast. After the brief encounter with the Indian captain nothing was going down my throat any more. In any case both of us had to get ready in the next fifteen minutes to board the team coach. There was little time left.

Through the tour I had sat on the last row of the bus. It

helped me get away from the glare and unwanted attention. As I sat in the last row, my mind was completely on the game ahead. I was visualizing what would happen if India batted first and the first wicket fell at 10. How would I react? It was cold and very windy. As the bus moved towards our destination, the sky started getting darker. It seemed to reflect my mind filled with anxiousness. I found myself thinking about two bits of invaluable advice I had received on the tour.

The first was from a batting maestro called Desmond Haynes. Haynes was then coaching Sussex. We were playing his county in Hove in a warm-up match just before the start of the one-day series. In those days an extra player was allowed to take part in the warm-up matches. I was in the eleven but at some stage had come out to make way for another player. This was just after tea. It suited me perfectly as I was looking for an opportunity to approach the great man.

Haynes was a role model of mine. He and Greenidge were a pair that would take apart any bowling attack in the world. From the start of the day's play I had kept a close watch on him. He was sitting in the Sussex dressing room, absorbed in the match. I worried that he might not take kindly to an impulsive young Indian cricketer barging in on him. He would not remember that four years ago I had played a one-day match against his West Indies at the Gabba.

Finally I gathered enough courage to approach him. Haynes quickly put me at ease and spoke as if I was a close relation. I asked him how I could manage the English weather. During the early part of the English summer the wickets remained damp and the ball swung more, and seamed considerably off the wicket. It made the Indian team especially vulnerable and our record in this season was pretty dismal.

Haynes gave me some advice that I'll never forget. He mentioned a few technical points – that in such conditions you had to be constantly on the front foot and needed to know where the off stump was. But mostly he dealt with mental preparation and its importance. This conversation took place about twenty-one years ago. Yet I will remember the Haynes discourse forever. Later I realized that he was teaching me about life. Not cricket.

Over to Haynes:

I played top-class cricket continuously for 15–16 years for a team that didn't know how to lose. What stood out in that team was enormous self-belief. The era had some outstanding and fearsome fast bowlers. Lillee, Thomson, Pascoe, Imran, Akram, Willis, Snow, Hadlee. To come through the challenge that they presented on the twenty-two yards, you had to be mentally very strong.

Every night before I went to sleep I would sit in the hotel room and go over my performance. I calculated how I would score the next day. I visualized that I would hit the fast bowlers in front of the wicket, through the cover region. And it happened exactly as I had imagined.

On the nights I was a bit apprehensive and thought I might offer an edge to Lillee at the Gabba, that invariably happened too. Seven times out of ten, cricketing successes are born out of visualizing positively. It doesn't matter whether a Lillee or a Pascoe is on the other side. If you are mentally prepared to score against them, chances are that you will. Eight times out of ten, failures happen because of surrendering mentally. A negative mindset will only bring in negative results.

I would remember that conversation with Haynes through my cricketing career. I could clearly see at that young age that winners handle pressure differently. While most people are paralysed by the thought of failure, champions think of pressure as an opportunity to climb further up the ladder.

Rahul was sitting near me in the bus as was the unputdownable Javagal Srinath, who would always crack jokes and keep us relaxed. But on that particular day the drive to Old Trafford was different. I was barely listening to Srinath.

As I played back Haynes's words, I also thought of a gentleman called Mark Craig. He was a psychologist assisting Worcester. I had met him very early in the tour while we were playing Middlesex.

Our game at Lord's was severely affected by the rain. The Worcester team had also arrived around the same time as they had a county game against Middlesex the next day. I knew a few of the Worcester players from before. They were training at the Lord's Nursery End. While the team was packing up in the dressing room I walked all the way to the Nursery End and asked my friends if I could spend fifteen minutes with their team psychologist. I had heard good things about him.

You have to understand the sense of urgency and desperation on my part here. I knew this tour offered me a last chance and that if I failed the nail would hammer down into my cricket coffin. Plus the negative talk around my selection gnawed at me. Run-scoring in the first half of the English summer has always been difficult. I was raw, somewhat immature and my low-key performance stressed me out.

I was also not sure if I would get the chance to play an ODI or a Test. With so many big names on the tour there was every possibility that I might go back not having played even one major game. I did not want a repeat of Australia. The voices in my head got louder and louder, filling me with anxiety and pessimism. I realized I needed some help.

My chat with Craig may not have lasted more than twenty minutes. He had to rush off to be with his county team. But every word he said was golden. I asked him, how can I handle so much pressure?

He said, pressure will always be there at the top level – from the day you face the first ball in your career to the last time you wear your whites. You have to find a way to deal with it and move forward. For this, you have to remain in the present. You can't afford to carry the past and worry about the future.

'Sourav,' he told me, 'as an athlete you can't control everything. You will always have external forces deciding your future, especially during your formative years. So the best way for you to approach the tour would be to play each and every game with equal intensity. Whether it is a side game or a Test, you must play with the same passion.

'You may not get 200 balls in an innings and get only 20. But try and give your best in that 20. If you manage to impress the management with that 20-ball innings, next time they will invite you for a bigger opportunity. Remember, in life small successes open up the door for bigger ones.'

He also gave me the example of a man sitting beside the river and fishing for a few days. 'He may look very relaxed from the outside but ask him how he feels after three–four days. He will come and tell you, Sourav, I would rather be in your world and not mine. The bottom line is, you will enjoy your holidays only when there is pressure in your work.

'What is life without any problems? What is a job without any pressure? Also remember every time you solve a problem internally you will only get better. Stronger. Smarter. It is almost like solving a puzzle. Once you do it, your confidence grows. If you say you are turning your back at a challenge because you fear the pressure, then you are wasting an opportunity to get better.'

I had already started playing deliveries sitting in the bus from the Manchester hotel to the Old Trafford cricket ground. I realized that it was not just a question of displaying proper technique. What was more important at that stage was putting my mind ahead of the unknown fears. On our way we passed a new Starbucks outlet, a trendy shopping mall, nightclubs and hangouts. But nothing registered in my mind.

I started visualizing Dominic Cork, England's spearhead,

who would do everything to put me off balance – bringing the ball back in, trying to hit my pad, sometimes pitching the ball away. Always trying to keep me on the back foot.

I was in my own world. Nothing registered. I noticed nothing including the tension that was brewing between the captain and Navjot Singh Sidhu. My mind was only on three individuals.

Chris Lewis

Darren Gough

Dominic Cork

Finally we reached the ground. I did my warm-ups. Practised a bit and stood in front of the wicket, waiting for Azhar to emerge for the toss. I wanted to ask the captain for advice but didn't have the guts to approach him.

He must have felt the same in 1985 when he was playing his first Test match. But 1996 was different for him. Today he was the boss, conducting an interview with nothing to lose. While I was only an applicant. At the age of twenty-three I was chasing a dream which could have gone either way based on that particular day. Yes, it was that crucial. That important.

Then I saw Azhar walking down the steps of the dressing room for the toss. I watched as the coin rose in the air and fell, and Mike Atherton picked it up. It was cold. There was a light drizzle making it all the more difficult to bat. I knew Atherton would put us in. That is what exactly happened.

India lost a wicket in the very first over. Cork went past Tendulkar and I walked out. Ideally I would have liked Tendulkar at the other end. His solidity and presence would have made batting a lot more easier for a newcomer like me. But then the Almighty upstairs had decided to test me in all possible ways. I finished with a confident-looking 46. But the impact of the 46 on me was far greater.

That day the ball swung heavily and seamed wildly, making it all the more difficult for batsmen from the subcontinent, who are unused to such conditions. I don't think I ever batted better in such challenging circumstances. I had some friends in the team. The Kumbles, the Dravids, the Sachins, friends I had played with at the junior level.

They seemed very happy for me. As I walked into the dressing room after getting out, I heard a few voices saying that my batting was superb.

India lost the match and we went back to the hotel. I had been so preoccupied with performing well that I hadn't noticed a battle had been brewing within the team. My roommate Sidhu had abandoned the match and gone home in disgust. A cricketer leaving like that during a tour and returning to India was unheard of. But I didn't get stressed. I was busy fighting my own war.

People talk about my Lord's hundred. But I would say the real defining knock was the 46 I scored at Old Trafford. It gave me a confidence that no other performance had. However elated I was, an inner voice also warned me that I couldn't afford to relax. It kept on saying, your test papers are only going to get tougher from here. Remember this, what you successfully cleared at Old Trafford was only the entrance.

How right the inner voice was I realized only later.

5

On to the Lord's Honours Board

I was sitting in one corner of the Lord's dressing room. Sachin walked over to me and put an arm around me affectionately. 'You relax. Have tea. I will put the tapes,' he said and began to fix the handle of my bat. I was not out and playing in full flow, interrupted only by the tea break. I had already scored an immensely satisfying debut hundred and was still looking good for some more. My bat handle had come loose in the long innings – a regular occurrence on away tours as the ball hits the splice of the bat because of the additional bounce on such pitches. This is what Sachin was offering to fix. The great Tendulkar's gesture might seem like a small one to you. But I knew it meant something more. It was a sign of appreciation, respect and a quiet welcome to the club of big boys.

The Old Trafford one-day knock had convinced me – rightly or wrongly – that the dream of earning my maiden Test cap was not far away. My performance in the match against Derbyshire had upped my chances even further. After the first Test match the Indian team had travelled straight to Derby where we were offered a green top, a pace bowler's paradise.

The star Aussie batsman Dean Jones was their overseas professional. But they also had in their ranks a fearsome quickie, perhaps then the fastest in England – Devon Malcolm. His partner was the aggressive Phillip DeFreitas. Their combination on that surface was lethal.

Tendulkar rested in the match. The great man had this tendency of picking up all kinds of gossip when he wasn't playing and he never missed an opportunity to create a stir in the dressing room. I must say the dressing room at the old Derbyshire ground was only slightly bigger than my drawing room. Even a whisper wouldn't escape anyone's ears.

Sachin had heard that this India game was a fitness test for Devon Malcolm. He was being vetted by the English selectors to play for England in the first Test. It meant that Malcolm was going to go flat out to impress them.

This caused panic in the Indian dressing room. If I had been more senior, I would have stopped Tendulkar by saying, Sach, don't spread unnecessary panic. You will be sleeping in the dressing room, but I will have to go at number 3 to play that red cherry coming out of his hands. In 1996 I was a rank junior and did not dare do so.

India crumbled in less than three days. The highest score of 81 came from a shy young man from Behala who was trying to spread his arms in Test cricket. I felt that after this performance my selection hopes increased substantially for the Lord's Test.

On the opening Test match of the series, the captain had left out an in-form batsman on a green top and played two spinners. We had three spinners on the tour which itself was a luxury. I felt I was absolutely ready but had to wait for my chance. A fear gripped me that if this combination worked I would perhaps have to sit out for the entire series.

Today twenty-one years after the incident my views are no longer the same. As you grow older you realize that as a youngster you may view a certain situation from your own angle but others might look at the same thing in a completely different way. It doesn't mean you have been wronged. It's just that you are a smaller player in larger negotiations and strategies.

India had lost the first Test and once again we were on the team bus to London. I had this huge ability to sleep in the bus and made sure I carried my pillow along and kept it on the last seat. During the trip, Ajay Jadeja walked up to me and said, 'By the time this tour finishes, you will be a star.' I looked at him and said nothing. I thought he was mocking me. I told myself how ironic his words were. Here I am not even considered good enough for a Test and he is saying that soon I'll be a star.

I looked at him and smiled and thought he was clever enough to understand my silence. We reached London and checked into the Holiday Inn Hotel, later renamed Danubius. The hotel is just across from Lord's. It is a wonderful place. You get up in the morning, pull open your curtains and the magnificent ground is right in front of you.

We were told to assemble at the Lord's dressing room around 9.45 a.m. There was no coach available and we had to walk on our own to the sporting ground. I finished breakfast, went to the back gate of the hotel, crossed St John's Wood Road and walked into the Mecca of cricket. As I walked past the iconic Grace Gate, I kept expecting the hawk-eyed Lord's stewards to stop me even though I was wearing the India tracksuit. Luckily they didn't.

After entering, I felt I had managed to get a job with the biggest company and had arrived for my first day in the office. I walked past the iconic Long Room, sat on those high chairs in the membership stands, then became a little worried that it might be meant for the members, that a steward might appear and ask me to leave.

There was no mobile camera in those days. No video option on a phone to record the moment. Yet even after so many years I can tell you exactly where I went, what I saw, which staircase I used.

I went to the nets not sure whether I would bat or bowl first. All of a sudden the visibly worried coach Sandip Patil approached me. He wore the sour expression of a coach who had not won a single game on this tour. But Sandy bhai's words were sweet. 'You are playing tomorrow and will bat at number 3,' he told me.

My head buzzed with excitement, Sandy bhai's voice faded out and I could barely hear him. I wanted to ask him some more questions but felt tongue-tied. My time had finally come. I could hardly believe it.

I felt huge excitement and energy. I was ready. A young man's mind at that age is the engine of a new Rolls-Royce which has not recorded even 10 kilometres. That engine is ready to hit any road fearlessly.

From a distance I saw the Indian openers padding up for the nets. They were Vikram Rathore and Nayan Mongia. It was clear that in this Test match the management would play around with the batting order. Mongia had never opened outside India. So effectively I was going to be the second opener. I realized that I could be in after the first ball of the day.

If a youngster asks me for advice before he approaches his debut Test match, I shall tell him, try not to think too much in advance. Try to be in the present. Believe in your talent. Let your instincts take over. Unconsciously I did exactly that in my Lord's innings.

Sitting here at my Behala residence I can still recapture my six-hour-long innings, with its three breaks, almost minute to minute. Every run gave me so much pleasure. Ask me where the 50th run came from while I was in a partnership with my captain. Where did I play my first off drive? I remember it all.

Very early in the innings England started their brand of sledging, which is only marginally different from Australia's – a bit of tongue-in-cheek with typical English sophistication and humour. Alec Stewart later became a dear friend. But he was sledging me constantly saying things like, 'Let's test him and see if he is good enough to play one more match.' I, however, remained unperturbed.

The England captain was Mike Atherton. Years later we played together for Lancashire and became close friends. Athers lives life at his own pace. We have travelled together and commentated for a number of matches. But in June 1996 I did not know him. So there was no conversation with him on the field.

To refresh your memory, India won the toss and asked England to bat. We had them on the ropes with 107-5 but Thorpe and Russell took them to a relative safety zone of 344. I came out to bat on the second afternoon after spending 130 overs on the field. Not to forget that I had bowled 15 overs as well and picked two important wickets of Nasser and Hick. My strong bowling added to my confidence.

That day, I finished overnight at 26 not out. I took off my pads and sat in one corner of the dressing room. I instantly started visualizing what I could have done better. I went to sleep exhausted and calm, ready for the next day.

The general thinking in cricket suggests breaks are not good as they break your rhythm. I would say there are no hard and fast rules. The next day at lunch I was still batting at 65. At Lord's, they arguably serve the best lunch in the cricketing world. The lunchroom is a separate arena outside the dressing room.

Since a huge landmark awaited me just 35 runs away, I was in no mood to get into a crowded lunchroom and risk even the slightest lapse in concentration. The twelfth man for the Test came running and was kind enough to ask, do you want me to get some lunch for you? I said, no thanks. I just wanted to be in the zone.

After the break, I watched every ball. I remained calm, not worrying about the next session or even the next over. My mind was always in the present. I was enjoying every moment. The hundred eventually came. I somehow felt I was destined to get past the milestone. The entire ground gave me a standing ovation and I was really touched.

While we were returning to the pavilion at tea, Dravid, my partner, let me go first. While I was going past the members' stand, they all stood up and clapped. When I was entering the dressing room, the entire team gave me a standing ovation. What a moment it was! After such a long wait, I could finally stretch my arms and say, international cricket, here I am.

A Lord's hundred was like no other hundred. It was the most hallowed cricket ground in the world. My name now would be permanently displayed on the iconic Lord's Honours Board alongside the names of players I had so admired. I had truly arrived.

My innings of 131 coming from 301 balls and Rahul's fighting 95 helped India to take a first innings lead. We could not manage a win but the first innings lead was a good psychological boost to the team that had not won anything on the tour.

PS: Tendulkar putting the bat tape for me was another unforgettable moment. It taught me that opinion about a new player changes in the team once he performs. But you can't expect them to respect you the very first day you walk into the dressing room. Respect takes time to build and earn, I realized that day. Important lessons, not just for cricket but for life.

6

Kolkata Celebrations and Toronto Bombshell

Trent Bridge has a lovely dressing room above the ground level. As I climbed the stairs leading up to it with Sachin during the tea break, I saw the Indian captain standing near the door, clapping his hands. Sachin was batting on 140. I was on 130. This was the third and last Test match of the series and we desperately wanted to level up. Azhar told me, wonderful work. I am going to gift you a watch.

At the beginning of the tour he had not believed in my abilities and had doubted my selection in the team. But all that changed with my performance. Azhar was honest enough to admit this and appreciate my performance.

I had no problems with that. All of us have fixed notions and opinions about certain players. All of us believe that a certain player will win for us while another won't. That comes from a word called faith and it's not personal. But when an underrated player shows that he is pretty good, honest captains quickly correct themselves. Azhar was no exception. It made our relationship stronger.

Azhar kept his promise and gifted me a sporty silver watch on the fifth day of the Trent Bridge Test match. It remains one of my most prized possessions. While I was clearly the in-form batsman along with Tendulkar, our captain had struggled with his batting. This country was considered Azhar's happy hunting ground and his Lord's hundred in 1990 remains the stuff of legends. When you keep getting runs you feel it will happen again, but form can be fickle and on that tour it deserted a very good player.

A continued bad run and losing both the Test and one-day series against England eventually cost Azhar the Indian captaincy. He was replaced after seven years by Sachin. I did not spend time thinking about these changes in Indian cricket. As a young player I was too busy charting my own course and trying to enhance my skills. Sachin was someone I had played with as a junior and I was proud to see his progress. We expected big from him. He was a big player.

As for me, after years of doubt and worry, I was feeling a little more confident after my successful outing in England. Sourav Ganguly – you, too, belong to this level. Every good performance instils in you a solidity, a quiet understanding that you are on a par with the best.

You know you have performed well; no one can take that away from you or make you believe otherwise. And it is from this that the truest, most unshakeable confidence arises. Something that can't be imparted, can't be instilled, can't be inspired. It is the work itself, the daily good performance, that rewards you.

I still remember the last few days of the England tour. My send-off was emotional and I received tremendous love and warmth from the Indians who lived in the UK. Animesh kaka threw a dinner party for me.

During my formative years when I was training in England he had been my sole anchor in the country. Now that all his efforts had culminated in success, he was like a proud father. He was addicted to cricket and to see one of his own succeed in the UK gave him a lot of joy. The couples who were invited to his residence that night had each cooked a dish for me. They all wanted to feed Sourav, they said.

It was a warm, happy evening, one I can never forget. In the smiling faces of the guests I could see genuine pleasure at my performance. My twin tons perhaps gave them an increased sense of belonging in Britain. My old coach Debu Mitra was also there. Debuda was a great source of inspiration and had guided me affectionately with my cricket till I played my first Test match.

While I was preparing to leave London, I got a call from home. My friends and relatives wanted to organize an open car reception for me once I landed in Kolkata. I said no. I felt a bit shy and with typical Bengali middle-class conservatism scoffed at the idea. I also felt that I should not get carried away. I wanted to be restrained but let's admit it I enjoyed every bit of the adulation. Typical, isn't it?

I landed in Kolkata. My father and members of the family were at the airport to receive me. I was so happy to see them. My family car drove me through the streets of Kolkata to my home at Behala, which was a good one and a half hour's drive from the airport. I was relieved not to see much fanfare at the airport but there was a surprise in store.

Halfway through the journey, as we reached the crowded north-eastern part of the city, I noticed that the windows along the streets were open and people were shouting from their houses. Hundreds of people appeared and surrounded my car. I was forced to get down and climb on to an open-roofed jeep.

There was genuine pride in their faces. I had become their own, their face to the world. The scene was incredible with more and more people joining the celebrations. Some handed me flowers. Some shook my hand. Others shouted, Bangalir chele biswodarbare gorbito korechey. A Bengali has made us proud on the world stage.

I felt overwhelmed. All the pain and the trouble I had undertaken had been worth it. I noticed an old lady trying to make her way through the crowd. She must have been over seventy. She could barely walk. Yet she had come to bless me.

Only two and a half months ago I had left for England in my family car, unnoticed, unannounced. And today this was happening to me! The venerable chief minister of Bengal, Jyoti Basu, had called to offer his congratulations in England. That was the first time I had spoken to him. A week later the CM's office would call again wanting to give me a state reception. Everything was different. Everything had changed.

Lots of people had gathered at my house, waiting to congratulate me. Someone had brought a big cake which I cut amid roars of laughter. Then I was faced with an attack much more menacing than the English bowling. My mother, Ms Nirupa Ganguly.

I was carrying three champagne bottles. These were given

72

to me for winning the Man of the Match and eventually the Man of the Series awards. I was a complete teetotaller, then and now, but my friends demanded that the bottles be opened right away and that I take a few sips.

My father had bailed me out in many delicate situations. This time he could be of no help. In a deeply religious family, led by my mother, even the strongest quaked in their shoes when it came to drinking.

My father used to hide his beer bottles in a secret place in the house where my mother had little chance of visiting. That night though the rules were broken. The bottles were uncorked with joy. My mother watched with her eyes glowing.

It turned out that the cable TV connection had gone off in the locality when I was batting at 90. My parents had invited a lot of people on the match day and the get-together had come to a standstill.

The suspense in my house must have been unbearable but perhaps it was for the best – my father was a heart patient and the tension might not have been good for him. Finally my uncle from London called home to tell my parents that I had reached the landmark. I was told my father laughed the whole evening.

I happened to be the second Bengali after Pankaj Roy to score a Test hundred and the city had erupted. I had little chance of resting that night as celebrations continued till the early hours of the morning. Kolkata also seemed to be partying.

People would stand outside my house waiting to take

an autograph or click a picture. All these years this part of India hadn't had much success on the cricketing map and once it did the cricket-loving masses just went crazy.

I started getting a few endorsements. The first one I signed was brought by Krish Srikkanth's agency. It was for Parry's toffees. Meanwhile a new life of attending functions and gracing occasions had already begun. ISKCON had called me to inaugurate their Rathyatra function.

Another special guest was the actress Hema Malini. I was a nervous twenty-three-year-old. I was so shy that I could hardly exchange any words with her. The film star Mithun Chakraborty had announced a cash award for me, which I said I would only accept if he came home. And he did. Our entire family sat with him for dinner and we laughed non-stop that evening.

Deep down I was getting a little worried. I knew the next innings would begin from zero and that top-level cricket was merciless. We had a short one-day series in Sri Lanka under the new captain, Tendulkar.

We played three one-dayers in Sri Lanka. In later years I played some of my best cricket in that beautiful country but on that trip I got demoted from my customary number 3 to number 7. I did manage to score a fighting 50 but I ought to have read the writing on the wall.

Toronto was next. The Indian board had decided that in Toronto the team would play a five-match one-day series annually with Pakistan called the Sahara Cup. I thought to myself that this tournament would provide me a good opportunity to showcase my talent.

After landing at Toronto, we drove down the beautiful motorway to the team hotel. It was my kind of world. This was no congested city. There was freshness in the air. Every time I have been in surroundings like this, I have felt a mental freedom.

I was asked to double up with Debashish Mohanty, who was my closest friend in the team. It is important that the roommate should be someone you are completely comfortable with. Debu, as I fondly called him, was that sort.

It was the first international cricket game in that part of the world. Matches were played at the ice-skating club which had a beautiful ground. Stands were temporary but accommodated 25,000 people. We were a little worried about the surface and knew the conditions would not be easy for batting. What made it even more challenging was that all five games would be played on one turf.

As the series got closer, we were down 1-2. On the morning of the third match wrenching news awaited me. I was informed that I had been kept out of the eleven and that Kambli would take my place. It was a shock but this was the professional sporting world. You are only as good as your last effort. Even in my wildest dreams I had not seen this coming.

I was dropped for the fifth game as well and Pakistan went on to win the series 3-2. I had a feeling that I might have to start all over again. I boarded the flight from Toronto in a confused state of mind. All sorts of negative thoughts came to my mind. Are they now going to drop me from Test matches? Hadn't I just scored back-to-back hundreds?

I was only twenty-four and my hard-won confidence still rested on weak scaffolds. I did not have the courage to ask the captain or the coach the reasons for my exclusion. The entire city of Kolkata had reacted very strongly to my being left out. Effigies were burnt and there had been a few unruly scenes against the captain and the coach. I was worried that they would think I had somehow instigated this.

I didn't know what to do but decided to stay quiet and let time do its work. When you are down and times are tough, the best solution is to work hard and keep quiet. Only your actions and nothing else can change your destiny.

So after returning to Kolkata I called up the captain. I apologized for the extreme behaviour of the people of my city and assured him that I had absolutely nothing to do with it. Luckily Sachin understood. I was honest with him, and our long association helped. He knew where I came from. He behaved like a leader.

Sandip Patil was removed as coach a few weeks after Toronto. Several years later I had a heart-to-heart with him in Mumbai. He was by then a close friend.

Sandy bhai said, 'Sourav, today I must apologize to you for what happened years ago in Toronto. I must admit my assessment of your cricketing abilities was wrong. I am very happy to see the way your career eventually progressed. But honestly, I never thought you would be so successful. I felt you were not strong enough mentally.'

I said to myself, all of us make mistakes in life. All of us make wrong assessments of others. It takes courage to own up to your mistakes and say sorry. My relationship with Sandy bhai grew even closer from that afternoon.

7

Bapi Bari Ja

I had watched star-struck as he bowled at Eden Gardens. I had followed his matches avidly on television, read as much as I could about him as a teenager. But it was only in 1997, at the Indian high commissioner's party in England, that I finally met the legendary Imran Khan.

I was super excited.

I was then going through a dip. The exclusion in Toronto the previous year had hurt me big time. And the Guyana Test match only added salt to the wound. In the West Indies I had scored in most of the matches, barring the Barbados Test match.

But I was dropped in the last Test match of the series to make place for an extra bowler. As in the past, the decision seemed inexplicable and left me anguished. I felt that on the slow West Indian tracks I would be a handy extra option with the ball.

My rational mind said, as it had in Toronto, that I should never take my place for granted at any time. But I have to admit that I found each of these rejections difficult to absorb, perhaps because I was new and inexperienced. But these helped me become tougher in the years to come.

I always believed that unless a young player gets the confidence and security to play over some time, he cannot perform at his best. Will he ever be relaxed enough for that? This was an issue I addressed when I became captain. Also, this was the first time I started believing in the title of this book, a century is not enough.

My stature in Bengal, meanwhile, had changed enormously. The local and the national media were extremely supportive. Countless fan mails arrived every day at home. I got noticed everywhere I went in Kolkata. But deep inside, I felt I was hardly the hero that I wanted to become.

Imran was very generous and friendly. He said, 'I have watched your batting. You are doing very well.' His warmth unlocked something in me, and I found myself listening avidly to his words. Imran said something I shall never ever forget. 'Sourav, you should only fly higher. When you fly in the sky and see dark clouds, the only way to negotiate is to fly higher. I have also been left out a couple of times so I know what it feels like. You just have to fly so high that your competition is left far behind. This is the only solution to your problem.'

Simple words with a simple meaning. But Imran had expressed the idea with so much conviction and authority that it had a terrific effect on me. I was instantly recharged. A few months later I became the hero of the nation in a sensational series where we thrashed Imran's country 4-1.

I scored 222 runs in the series and bagged 15 wickets and the Man of the Series title. What a massive turnaround it was. Imran's words had acted like a mantra, and I thanked him silently. A young cricketer, uncertain and troubled, had found a new perspective to the game and maybe even life.

Before I talk about my exploits against Pakistan in Toronto in September 1997, it is only fair that I take you to Jaipur where it all began. It was one of those relatively relaxed yet intense afternoons before the start of the tri-series. My phone rang in the hotel room. It was captain Tendulkar. And he was urgently calling me to his room.

Life has taught me that the best things in life happen in an unplanned fashion. That day in Jaipur, Sachin calmly informed me that I would have to open in the tri-series. It didn't matter whether I agreed or not. He had clearly made up his mind.

The series was beginning in just two days and involved the strongest nations, South Africa and Australia. That I had previously never opened in any of the representative matches only added to my worries.

In fact, I wasn't totally convinced of Sachin's decision. But he was my captain and I accepted the directive without any argument. I told myself that I had often played at number 3 in Test matches and that sometimes involved going in to bat in the first over. So what was new?

Two days later my journey as a one-day opener began and I didn't disappoint by scoring a stroke-filled 65. In one-day cricket I have never looked back. By the time I boarded a flight to Toronto, I had already scored my first one-day hundred in Sri Lanka as an opener. I was getting accustomed to that role very fast.

Today I can say with conviction that I wouldn't have been half the player if I had not been promoted at that stage. It was because of my own experience that I would later elevate Sehwag from the middle order to an opening slot so confidently.

The trauma of being left out the year before in Toronto still rankled. I was determined to reset my record in that venue. This has happened to me countless times in my career.

I remember in Bengaluru getting booed as the captain when we lost to Pakistan in the last Test match of the 2004 series. The next time we played Pakistan at Chinnaswamy, I was the toast of the crowd. I had scored a big double century against the likes of Shoaib Akhtar. The boos turned into cheers.

The conditions in Toronto were quite challenging, compared to the last time we had played here. Now it wasn't a dust bowl but a green top that welcomed us. Pakistan had a daunting pace bowling line-up comprising Aaqib Javed, Abdul Razzaq, Mohammad Akram and their newest sensation Mohammad Zahid.

The formidable Wasim Akram had to opt out because of an injury. Waqar was also unavailable. But handling Aaqib, I knew, would be tough in these conditions. I had also watched on TV Mohammad Zahid bowl against the great Brian Lara in Australia six months ago. I remembered what Lara said after the match – that Zahid was the quickest bowler he had faced in a very long time.

As I finished the last practice session and was getting my kit ready, my mind returned to the lows of the past year. I promised myself that by the time this series got over I would erase the unfortunate memories of the venue.

Having examined the pitch, I was convinced that in such conditions I would be a viable 10-over bowling option. Mental calculations told me if I bowled well I would get all five games as a batsman.

The batting was a huge struggle as the ball initially swung quite a bit and made movements off the wicket too. As I had anticipated, my bowling came to the rescue. By the time the second game ended we were 2-0 up in the series. In those two games I had picked eight wickets. It so turned out that Debashish Mohanty and I were the two hardest bowlers to negotiate on that surface. Aaqib and Fazal were much easier to handle.

The matches were so tense that sledging was rampant. Moin Khan from behind the stumps would taunt our batsmen, sometimes even abusing us. When things did not go their way the Pakistani pacers were at their eloquent best. Their batsmen also joined in.

I had got Salim Malik out in the earlier match. In the third game, while I was walking out to bat, he came up to me and threatened to take me to the cleaners: 'Aaj main tujhe itna marunga ki tu sirf dekhte rehna.'

As luck would have it, I got Malik out again. This time he was caught by Tendulkar and could score only 6. The Sourav Ganguly of later years would have returned Malik's compliment and made a strong parting comment. But I was pretty young then and could not muster enough courage to say anything to Pakistan's star batsman.

From my run-up I could see Malik walking away with a chuckle. I also got Rameez Raja out a couple of times in that series. Rameez was their captain and did not play for Pakistan again. Even today he jokingly reminds me whenever we meet that I am responsible for his exit from the Pakistan team.

I also made a lasting friendship with another left-handed opener on that tour. Saeed Anwar and I gelled effortlessly and spent lots of time together. I was a big admirer of his game. He was so gifted and could score effortlessly. I have never seen anyone play Srinath with so much authority and conviction.

But for me the incident that stands out in that Toronto series centred on Saeed's colleague Inzamam-ul-Haq. While walking out to open the innings, I saw Inzamam move himself from first slip to third man. It struck me as odd as I had not seen Inzamam field in that position.

It turned out that Inzy had been heckled through the Pakistan innings by a man in the audience with a megaphone. He had spotted the offender and changed his position to be near him. None of us were prepared for what followed. From deep third man, Inzy ran into the crowd and attacked that man. Play stopped for quite some time. It was all very colourful.

India had played with so much precision and courage in the series that Pakistan did not know what hit them. From this time onward Pakistani cricketers developed an unwavering professional respect for me. Later they would grudgingly tell me, we feared the match-winner in you more than we did any other Indian cricketer.

I still fondly recall walking into the press conference in Toronto with a relieved Indian captain after our second win. Sachin was eloquent about me at the conference, describing me as a man with the golden arm. Sitting next to him, I realized that I was being seriously viewed as an important member of the side. I can't tell you how great the feeling was.

The year before in the same country I had been genuinely worried about my future. Now the captain made me feel as if I was his most trusted man. I had to almost pinch myself to make sure this was happening.

We went on to win two of the remaining three matches of the series and my form remained lethal. After four one-dayers, I was sitting pretty with three Man of the Match awards. The last game was the most important as I thought the team management might get unpredictable if I underperformed. Well, I got a 96 in that game.

Not only was I declared the Man of the Series but I won a car as well. It was an Opel Astra. My standing as a cricketer went up several notches after this. Every Indian loved seeing Pakistan thrashed and I was seen as the hero of that victory.

The biggest difference between the young player who returned to his Behala residence heartbroken and the one who excelled this time was his mind. I was no longer tentative. When I felt relaxed, batting was like a joyride. I was a completely different player. Imran's and Haynes's advice was very much on my mind. How right they had both been.

Young cricketers reading this must understand that most of the game is played in your mind. You can spend hours and hours perfecting your technique at the nets but no doors will open for you until you have sorted the issues in your head and can deal with pressure. Don't run away from the tough stuff.

Heroes are made when you confront an uncomfortable situation head-on. Have you ever heard of a hero who sits at home, goes to office in the late afternoon after having slept for ten hours and finally ends the day going for an evening show?

After the hugely morale-boosting Toronto victory we hosted New Zealand at home. My form continued and I was once again the Man of the Series and won a brand new Fiat. This was the third car that I had won in six months.

Apart from the cars I also won a title from a man called Geoffrey Boycott. He started calling me the Prince of Kalkuta. The name stuck with me through my career even though the pronunciation of the city's name changed. As a commentator for Star Sports Geoffrey had admired my batting in my inaugural series. We didn't cross paths in England but would later meet and become close.

In Toronto he had come as a commentator for ESPN. One day while we were having breakfast together at the hotel I asked if I could discuss batting with him. He nodded. Geoffrey has a reputation for being unapproachable and a little aloof but I found him a lot friendlier than most people. Perhaps he took more time to open up. My experience suggests once he trusted a person he went all out for him.

I also found him extremely sound in his cricketing knowledge. For an English opener of the 1970s to score more than 8000 runs with an average of 47 demanded top-class technical skills.

Geoffrey's technical observations were so good that when I became captain I was extremely keen on roping him as a batting consultant. Sadly it didn't work out. While Geoffrey gave me that Prince tag he had conferred the King tag on Jagmohan Dalmiya. Mr Dalmiya by then had become president of the International Cricket Council (ICC) and Geoffrey called him the King of Kalkuta.

Now my first World Cup was nearing. I was getting super excited on two counts. One, that I would be competing on the biggest cricketing stage of the world. Two, my favourite country outside India was hosting it – England, the country that had never let me down.

During this period Indian cricket was going through a silent transformation. The Indian board had employed, for the first time, a foreign physiotherapist named Andrew Kokinos. Apparently this was done at the insistence of Bobby Simpson, who had joined the team for the 1999 World Cup as technical consultant.

People always talk about my disputes with Australian coaches. That's only partially true. With Bobby Simpson, for instance, my relationship was remarkable. Not only did he take me under his wing but he was instrumental in getting me my first county stint with Lancashire. Simpson has rated me as one of the best slip fielders he has seen.

He also brought in a completely new regime, an altogether different culture. Anshuman Gaekwad was the coach then. Anshu bhai complemented Simpson very well. A new work ethic began to be created in the Indian team, one which I had not experienced before. I began to wake up early in the morning, and went out for runs in our base in Leicester. By the time the tournament started, the fitness routine began to pay rich dividends.

Azhar was back as captain but he hardly made any difference as the template had been created by the coaches. I used to discuss these issues with Rahul regularly – we were on the same page concerning these new methods, believing this was the only way the Indian team could take the next leap forward. A few years later I became captain and Rahul the deputy. The environment we tried to create in the team had a lot to do with how we spent those two months leading to the World Cup.

I was extremely eager to do well in my first World C up. In the lead games I didn't get runs. I was probably too keen and went overboard. On the positive side, this made me very hungry when the real matches began.

Our first outing was against South Africa at Hove. It was a different South Africa then. With Pollock, Kallis, Klusner and Donald, the team presented, arguably, the best bowling line-up of the tournament. I was so nervous about Hove that I couldn't sleep all night.

On a seaming pitch, the South Africans bowled their hearts out. Despite the challenges, Sachin and I fought our way through to a century partnership. It was a tough opening game and we ought to have won it. If missing a century by four runs in my maiden World Cup match was not disappointing enough, coming so near to winning the match and failing hurt badly.

Despite batting so creditably, I heard a few murmurs about my performance. Some were blaming the loss on me for getting run out at such a crucial stage, an allegation I found outrageous. But by then I was more mature. I knew a top-quality professional had to deal with such noise.

We lost our second game against Zimbabwe. It was a shocking result. None of us expected it. To make things worse, Sachin had to go back to India as his father had died. Things were suddenly looking really bleak for India. We did a huge post-mortem in the dressing room after our defeat. In India, fans were outraged and upset. They were worried that the team might not qualify for the Super Six.

We had two back-to-back matches against Sri Lanka and England. We desperately needed to win both to qualify. We reached Taunton to play the defending champions, Sri Lanka. The ground was looking immaculate. I felt a charge while entering the Taunton cricket ground. We had grown up on the cricketing folklore of Viv Richards and Ian Botham. Many of these unforgettable county matches were played on this ground.

Sitting in the dressing room, I could feel the team was a bit edgy. A loss here would really open up the possibility of an early exit. And that would be such an anticlimax. Little did I know that the next day I would be breaking Kapil Dev's sixteen-year-old record for the highest individual score by an Indian in a one-day match.

After the match I remembered the day Kapil had scored 175 at Tunbridge Wells. While Kapil was hitting the Zimbabwe bowlers out of the park I was flying kites from my rooftop. Of course I had kept the transistor nearby and on maximum volume. My concentration was divided between winning a kite war in the Behala sky and a rampaging Kapil Dev a few thousand miles away.

Kapil had played, effectively, all by himself in that historic match. In my case I had a solid partner in Dravid. After the early dismissal of Sadagopalan Ramesh, it was Dravid who started playing aggressively. He was scoring at a rate of more than a run a ball. Then I caught up very fast. Between the two of us, Dravid completed his century first. There was great anticipation and suspense on the ground as I approached Kapil's record. Finally, I got past him.

Mohinder Amarnath, one of the 1983 heroes, happened to be at the match. I felt very proud that I had achieved this feat in the presence of Jimmy paaji, whom I have always admired as a tremendous player of fast bowling. In the evening, the hotel operator connected a call to my room. It was none other than the mighty Kapil Dev with his congratulations.

Taunton has always been a happy hunting ground. The wicket is pretty batting-friendly and has often been lucky for me. Playing my first county match for Lancashire against Somerset, I had scored a hundred here. I also played here in later years and don't think I failed even once.

After the match, our team was on its way to Birmingham. We had to play England there. However, I was returning to London for a day. Animesh Mukherjee and his immediate family had driven all the way down from London. I decided to return with them and rest for the night. So there I was, after the match, buckling up for a three-and-a-half-hour car ride. But mentally I was in such a peaceful state that I did not feel exhausted.

The next game was at Edgbaston. The expectation of the Indian supporters following Taunton had again reached sky-high. Conditions were vastly different compared to the last match. The sky remained cloudy and the ball swung relentlessly. I batted well again but due to rain the match got rolled over to the next day.

On the second day, conditions remained almost the same. At one point, it got so cold that it reminded me of Toronto in September. This time my bowling decided the fate of the match as I claimed 3 for 20, accounting for two dangerous English batsmen, Nasser Hussain and Neil Fairbrother. Nasser, a reliable number 3 batsman, had opened in that innings and scored a gritty 33 before I got him bowled.

I was handed over the second successive Man of the Match award and with it came another champagne bottle. I couldn't have asked for a better run in my maiden World Cup. Everything was going my way. I was hailed as the most important match-winner of the side alongside the great Tendulkar.

That the award was handed over by one Ian Terence Botham made it all the more special. He is truly a free spirit, and has a remarkable eye for the game. A few years ago I took part in a charity walk with him in Kandy. It was a eight-hour-long walk. Sir Ian was sixty then but walked so briskly that Sunil Gavaskar and I could not get near him. I marvelled at how fit he was. As you can tell, I am a bit of a fan boy. So you can imagine what it was like in Edgbaston in 1999. It was like a fairy tale, except my story didn't have a happily-ever-after ending.

The second day of the match at Edgbaston was played in slippery conditions because of the overnight rain. It had got very cold as well. It was only the seventh over of the day when my mud-covered spikes got stuck at the popping crease. I heard a click in my left leg. The pain began almost instantly. But I knew I had to bowl through it. It was a do-or-die game for us.

We won the match and qualified for the Super Six. But in the process I injured myself further. Each time my left foot fell on the crease as I bowled, the pain doubled. As soon as the match ended, our physio Dr Ravinder Chadda got straight to work on me.

Important matches were coming up and I knew I must get fit as soon as possible. Now if you are even slightly connected with sports you will know that injuries take time to heal when it is cold. The UK during that week was passing through a cold phase, which didn't help my case.

The Pakistan game was in Manchester. I was extra keen on playing this match having thrashed them ten months ago in Toronto almost single-handedly. I took a couple of injections thinking the shortcut route would ensure speedy recovery.

Because of the heated Kargil war with Pakistan, the match assumed extra significance. I must thank Dr Chadda here. He took extra care of me and remained very attentive. I knew how desperately some of my teammates wanted me to play. Sadly I couldn't. Forget running. I could barely walk. So I had to pull out of the Manchester match. My teammates, however, displayed great fighting spirit and beat Pakistan.

Around this time I heard a few murmurs regarding my injury – that I was faking it and that I had intentionally opted out of the Pakistan match. I was very disappointed to discover this. Although I didn't hear it directly and no one from the team management ever told me anything.

But as it happens in Indian cricket the real mischief-makers always exit through the back gate. They quietly pass comments, instigate others and then move away. I have always believed that injuries are best known to the players. An outsider will never give you the right picture.

My own experience suggests it is very hard for an artist to combat false allegations as he or she is untrained to fight such mean-minded gossip. And the allegations are often so petty and nasty that you can fall sick just by hearing them. Forget the intensity of my injury, I was thinking how on earth the doubters had forgotten my recent records against Pakistan. I knew public memory was short. But this short? By then I had become mentally a lot tougher. I just ignored them and the rumours died down.

My next hundred in international cricket happened pretty soon after the World Cup. These were almost back-to-back hundreds – against a menacing Glenn McGrath on a wet Melbourne wicket, and the formidable two Ws, Wasim and Waqar, in Adelaide.

Ask any batsman from that era how tough negotiating Akram with an old ball was. At times he seemed unplayable. I played him first in the Chennai Test match. He got Dravid out with the old ball and I was the next batsman in. The ball was swinging both ways and I felt completely at sea. I could also barely see his hand as he used to hide the ball between his palms beautifully.

I went up to my partner and captain Azhar, who was at the non-striker's end. I said to him, you are at least in a position to watch his hand more closely. If you see him delivering keeping the shine of the ball on the right, please lift your bat to the right. If you see him keeping the shine on the left, raise your bat with the left hand. I will adjust by looking at you.

This worked very well for a while until Moin Khan tipped off Wasim. He lost his temper, hurled a few abuses at me and retaliated with a bouncer. He was never easy for a batsman. Even on a free-flowing Adelaide track, Wasim was the Pakistani bowler I respected the most.

For a right-handed batsman he brought the vicious inswinger. And for me, he took it outside the off stump. Wasim swung both ways, presenting additional problems. Handling Waqar was comparatively easier.

A hundred against Wasim in the triangular series in Australia felt like a real achievement. Indeed, a hundred against him anywhere in this universe always earned you extra praise. This time it came from an emotional Kapil Dev in the Adelaide dressing room. Kapil paaji was then our coach. I had scored 141 off 144 balls and India won the match. I walked away with the Man of the Match award yet again.

The victories made me both angry and excited – and I dedicated these two fighting hundreds to my doubters. I always felt life was not about taking things lying down. Life is all about bouncing back. In the Kolkata maidan parlance a war cry is uttered while demolishing an argument.

Bapi bari ja.

Bapi is the imaginary white ball that the attacker steps out of the crease for and lifts on to the stands. With these knocks I was sending the same message to my critics, Bapi bari ja!

Part Two

Becoming a Leader

8

Demoted from Vice Captaincy, Promoted to Captaincy

I was busy stretching in one corner of Wankhede when I spotted coach Kapil Dev walking towards the middle of the field. As Kapil paaji walked past me, he whispered, 'Sourav, the selectors are considering you for captaincy.'

The entire nation knew that the fate of Indian captaincy was about to be decided in the next few hours in Mumbai. I didn't react to Kapil paaji's words. I didn't want the outside world, and that included the coach, to see my emotions as I'd heard such rumours earlier only for the official announcement to have turned out different.

Sachin Tendulkar had just given up the captaincy under excruciating circumstances. Sachin said nothing publicly but the reason was obvious. It was clear that the captaincy was affecting his batting. He also felt that certain decisions were being made around the team without consulting him. The truth perhaps lay somewhere in between.

As the vice captain I knew I was the natural successor but it would have looked very crude if I had openly expressed my interest. Then there was the mini scandal of last year – when my name was suddenly struck off from vice captaincy even after getting finalized. There is an age-old saying which I firmly believe in – in Indian cricket you can truly never count your chickens until they hatch.

The incident happened during the Asian Test Championships involving India, Pakistan and Sri Lanka. We were playing Pakistan at Eden Gardens. On day three of the Test match I read in the papers that my name was being considered for vice captaincy because of the consistency I had displayed in the last three years at the international level.

On day four, I had to pad up early as I was the not-out batsman. As I was getting ready, a selector came up to me and confirmed the newspaper report. I was very happy, and felt this was a very proud moment in the career of any cricketer.

When I reached home at about seven that evening, I learnt that Anil Kumble has been appointed the new Indian vice captain. I was surprised but felt happy for Anil. It didn't affect me too much. Later I was told the selectors did select me as the vice captain but Mr Raj Singh Dungarpur had struck down my name. Raj bhai, as we called him, was a very powerful figure in the BCCI and was the acting president of the body.

Ashok Malhotra was the East Zone selector. He had pushed my case for vice captaincy and had been upset at the manner in which their committee's recommendations were set aside by the president. He seemed more disappointed than I was.

A few rumours surfaced about Raj bhai's decision. One newspaper in Kolkata ran a story that he was not happy with my food habits. I found that outrageous but didn't care to find out the real reasons. Who would have known that I would become the deputy's boss in a year's time!

But let's rewind a bit. After playing Pakistan, we had gone to Sri Lanka. I have a soft spot for the island country which I have always found very warm and friendly. We were there almost every August–September and the Colombo Taj Samudra had become a home.

The Sri Lankan team in those days was in a vastly different league from the one you see today. We had two special tormentors – Sanat Jayasuriya and Aravinda de Silva – but the other players were also very good.

Sri Lanka in the late 1990s was going through huge political turmoil. Security at the picturesque Taj Samudra was very tight. Off the field we knew we were safe. But it was a different matter on the field, especially when a Jayasuriya or an Aravinda was in full flow. In 1997 Sri Lanka created a world record of 956 runs against us. Yours truly took Jayasuriya's catch but only after he had scored 340.

We were absolutely helpless – we tried all kinds of strategies, but nothing worked. Jayasuriya continued to decimate our bowling. One day we decided to try something new to break the shackles. It was decided to hold the team meeting, led by captain Tendulkar, sitting in the corridors of our hotel floor. The security made sure that no one entered the passage. We decided to have some snacks here and conduct a post-mortem.

The game plan centred on containing a raging Jayasuriya. We analysed his scoring shots and weak points. Our idea was to block his run-scoring zones and in the process make him impatient. Venkatesh Prasad was given this responsibility. We felt Operation Jayasuriya was highly possible if Venky made minor adjustments in his length. We charted out the possible catching areas as well. It was very comprehensive. For the first time we felt a glimmer of hope. Finally our days of toiling under the hot Sri Lankan sun would come to an end!

The next morning Venkatesh bowled to him as planned, a delivery which pitched on the good length. Jayasuriya flicked that over the square leg boundary on to the stands. It was almost ridiculous and the fielders actually started laughing. I have never seen such helplessness on a cricket field.

I particularly remember his triple century stand with Roshan Mahanama at the Khettarama (now Premadasa) stadium. During the partnership most of the time I was either at short leg or at silly point. Dravid and I alternated between the close in positions.

Jayasuriya must have employed more than 40 sweep shots in his innings. And every time I evaded the ball, as I feared that my shin bone would fracture while attempting the catch and I'd be out of the game for a long time.

We had three spinners in Anil Kumble, Rajesh Chauhan and Nilesh Kulkarni. Jayasuriya treated them all with equal contempt. Dravid and I were clearly in the danger zone – Jayasuriya's lethal hits could have really hurt us – and after each slog sweep we would exchange helpless glances and weak smiles with each other.

Nilesh Kulkarni was my roommate. The day before he had been jumping with joy as the Indian innings had finished slightly short of 550. Then he got Atapattu early in the Sri Lankan reply. That was Nilesh's first Test wicket and Sri Lanka were 39-1. At the end of the second day Nilesh seemed very happy and confident as we had coffee in the room. I was also hoping my roommate would run through the innings.

But Nilesh's optimism didn't last. In fact if you look at the final scorecard, I ended up bowling better than him with 2-53. (That incidentally was Mahela's first Test match and I accounted for him.) Poor Nilesh ended up with 1-195.

I still remember his face when he stormed into our hotel room at the end of the match. Usually docile, he was red-hot with anger. He fumed in his native Marathi, 'Tujhi aila [your mother's] . . . Yeh Jayasuriya ko kaise out kiya jaye?' Poor Nilesh. He never played for India again.

Six months after our Sri Lanka tour, I was appointed vice captain of India on the tour to Australia. The decision was taken in Ahmedabad. We were playing New Zealand, where I got a hundred in that test against Stephen Fleming's team.

Overall I had performed well in the series. In the Gwalior one-dayer I got an unbeaten 153 off 150 balls. We scored 262 and they could not get past 247. I had bowled 10 overs as well and picked up a few wickets and was declared the Player of the Match.

Yet after the match there was a bit of a showdown. Some players felt I should have played faster. Our coach, Kapil Dev, kept quiet during the argument that followed. Luckily, captain Tendulkar came to my rescue.

Since he had opened the batting with me he knew how

difficult it was to accelerate on that track. He also knew that since the first three wickets had fallen quickly I had to rebuild the innings.

In a week's time we were on our way to Australia having defeated New Zealand in both the one-day and the Test series. We had to compete against the best team of our era on their own turf. For the second warm-up match the captain took a break and asked me to lead. The match was against New South Wales in Sydney. I was pretty excited and a little anxious as well. I missed a hundred in that match but in both innings I was the highest scorer of the team.

The match saw the debut of two players who would go on to have glittering careers – Michael Clarke and Brett Lee. Brett had a Bruce Lee effect on the Indian batsmen as he took seven wickets in the match and impressed the Aussie selectors. We went on to win the game – as it turns out, this was our only victory against an Australian team on that tour.

I had led India previously at the Coca-Cola Singapore Challenge tournament against the West Indies as Sachin had rested due to a sore back. I had also led India at Toronto in a full series against Lara's West Indies.

But this was during a tour and that too in Australia. It had to be different. My idea of captaincy was practical, fearless and aggressive. My efforts were higly applauded by our coach. He would eventually have a big say in my appointment as the Indian captain.

The Test series was a complete disaster – we were simply washed away by a super talented team. It was very disappointing. I got a few fifties in the Tests and then had an outstanding triangular series – got a hundred against Australia in Melbourne and played a match-winning knock against Pakistan in Adelaide.

But all our individual efforts didn't add up. To be brutally honest, at that time our generation of players did not know how to win matches outside the subcontinent. Also, we did not have the bowling attack to get 20 wickets. However, the failure in Australia was a huge learning experience for me. I realized we were way behind as a team in overseas conditions. And that we needed to get better.

We came back to India and had our series scheduled against South Africa. Suddenly Tendulkar decided that enough was enough. He wanted his term as captain to end after the two Test match series against South Africa as he felt that leading the team was affecting his batting.

I will be completely honest here. The moment Sachin announced his decision, my hopes soared. Tell me, who doesn't want to be the Indian cricket captain? Isn't that the most coveted job after the Indian prime minister? Moreover I was the deputy. I thought I had a good chance as I had just had a good series and since Kapil Dev believed in me.

India lost the first Test. The selectors were due to announce the team and the captain for the one-day series in Mumbai. I remembered what had happened in Kolkata a year ago and told myself, be happy with what you have got. There are things you won't be able to control in life and it is not sensible obsessing about them.

That evening a journalist friend called me excitedly in my hotel room at the Taj. 'Please turn on the television. They have appointed you as the captain.' I turned on the TV and saw my name in the headlines. Almost three years and eight months after my Lord's debut, I had become captain of the Indian cricket team. If someone had told me when I was fourteen, one day you will become the Indian captain, I would have told them to stop pulling my leg.

It was the happiest day of my life. Dona, who was travelling with me, had never ever interfered with my cricket. Even on a tour she allowed me enough space to remain focused. This time she seemed equally elated.

I was asked by the BCCI to take part in a press conference. It was unusually long and went on for forty-five minutes. The experience was surreal. The flashbulbs exploded in my face. I was short of words. I was careful too to mask some of my joy since the captaincy was being given to me under the shadow of Sachin's decision. I didn't want to appear insensitive. But I doubt if I managed to conceal my happiness from the media.

Even after the press conference I was on cloud nine. It was like a fairy tale – especially since my journey to cricketing success had come with so many difficulties, so many rejections. I kept pinching myself to make sure that, yes, I was indeed captain of India. That this was not a dream.

The first thing I did next morning was walk up to Sachin and spend nearly half an hour with him. I said, you were the one responsible for my growth and development as a cricketer. I owe a lot to you. You will continue to be the most important member of this side and a leader who will take the game forward along with me. He assured me of his help.

When I entered my maiden selection committee meeting

as the newly appointed captain, the first thing the selectors asked me was who my preferred choice for the vice captain was. Without batting an eyelid I said Dravid. He and I shared the same vision for the team. Some eyebrows were raised as Dravid was not known as the fastest one-day bat. But I was certain that only he fitted the bill.

I started my Test career with Rahul, even played a bit of junior cricket with him. He was inscrutable, always calm. A pleasure for any captain to work with and a role model for youngsters wanting to become top-level batsmen. I knew we would make a good team.

My examination began in Kochi. Before I went out to address my first team meeting I had called my wife to say I was feeling a bit nervous. Usually I didn't trouble her with cricketing matters but that day was different.

Essentially I was a shy person who found it difficult to open up in a gathering. Two former captains of mine sat in that meeting. My introverted nature had also rubbed some of my team members the wrong way. I knew that I had to make an impression. Also I wanted to set the tone from the very first ball. I didn't want to wait and delay the reforms which were so desperately required.

I was aware too that we were at a very critical stage in Indian cricket. We had had a spate of defeats and all kinds of stories were circulating in the media. Some involved the team and a few particular players. The dark days of the match-fixing era was slowly being revealed. The unit was battered and demoralized. It was not easy to lift the team from this slump. I knew my job was going to be very tough. Later I realized heroes were created out of such situations.

Many well-wishers and journalist friends gifted me the classic Mike Brearley book, *The Art of Captaincy*. I mean no disrespect to the book or Mr Brearely, whom I admire a great deal, but books or team meetings don't make you good captains. For me, the art of captaincy was not theory but practice. I wanted to chart my own way and create a new template for success.

One, I wanted the team to perform well overseas. Two, I wanted to change the body language and attitude of the team. I had observed the body language of overseas captains and players and thought we must replicate the same.

I always thought we were a collection of quality individuals but in high-pressure moments we all fell apart. I wanted to build a new team culture quickly. The coach was on the same page as me and allowed me to effect the changes.

I was inspired by the way the Aussies played their cricket. I wanted to inculcate the same spirit in my team. I was very clear in my mind that I would only play to win. And while attempting to win if I lost I didn't mind. I wanted to create a culture of winning and absolutely detested draws.

My first assignment was to take on Hansie Cronje's South Africa in Kochi. I had a lot of respect for Hansie – a captain who wouldn't concede an inch. When the fixing stories and his involvement came to light, I was stunned. The South African team he led was one of their all-time top teams. Even in Indian conditions they had steamrolled us in the Test series.

The first match of the one-day series was very vital – as much a mental battle as it was with the bat and the ball.

Powered by Ajay Jadeja's 92, we managed to win by three wickets. The next match was in Jamshedpur. Sachin had departed early but I was in good nick and scored a hundred at a blistering pace to take it away from the Proteas.

My brother Snehasish was in the stands. It was his pursuit of cricket that had led me to the game so it was particularly pleasing that he could witness my hundred from the stands. Our Jamshedpur happiness didn't last long as the visitors retaliated aggressively in Faridabad. Despite my half-century Hansie took the match away from us and was deservedly named the Man of the Match.

Hansie would not have known that he was playing his last series for South Africa. With the series 2-1 in our favour, we managed to get past them in Vadodara and clinch the tournament. In the series-winning one-dayer I got 87. The Player of the Match was Sachin, who scored a masterly hundred. You could see the resolve and single-mindedness of a man who had left his crown, but had now set his goals higher.

Buoyant after the win, we went to Bangladesh to play the Asia Cup – my first international Test as captain. We didn't fare well but there was more serious news to overshadow our result. The Delhi Police had unearthed a match-fixing scam – phone calls had been recorded where a 'deal' had been discussed. The player was identified as Hansie. All hell broke loose. Cricket was never the same again.

Sitting at the posh Sonargaon hotel in Dhaka, we were engulfed in speculation, rumour and gossip. It was a terrible time. A month later in May, Kapil Dev came under fire following allegations made against him by a former player.

I felt sad to see him suffer – he would later break down and cry on national television – for he had played an important and generous role in my career.

While bad news was drowning Indian cricket and making undesirable headlines, my deputy and I were a few thousand miles away in England playing county cricket. We had both flown to England from Bangladesh.

Of course one kept track of the news but it was not the same as when you are in India. Remember this was the pre-YouTube–Internet era. It was while I was in England that I was told that our coach wanted to end his term because of how upset he was by the scandal. So the new captain needed a new coach. A quality coach.

I later read newspaper reports suggesting that Raj Singh Dungarpur was instrumental in bringing John Wright as the new Indian coach. This was anything but true. John's name was first suggested by Rahul. He was coaching Kent, where Rahul played as an overseas professional.

Rahul and I met again when Lancashire, my county team, played Kent. After competing on the field, we caught up at an Indian restaurant where we discussed our team rebuilding. Rahul mentioned John, who he was very impressed with. At Rahul's insistence I had a meeting with John and immediately took a liking to him. This is how his name came to be recommended to the BCCI. I thought history was created when John took over the Indian team. He introduced a new culture of fitness, bringing in a fitness expert and a trainer. It reshaped Indian cricket.

John and I had a big job on our hands. All of us knew the game's credibility had hit rock bottom and that we needed to turn it around. The team needed to get away from the match-fixing blues. It was a huge, huge scandal and was everywhere. In newspapers, on television, on hoardings. The country seemed to be talking only about the scandal. It seemed as if the ordinary Ram and Shyam had lost faith in cricket and cricketers.

As for me I was never approached by a bookie. I asked Rahul and some other seniors. They said they had never been approached either. So I had doubts about how widespread it had really been. The one good thing that came out of this was that the young players in the team realized what a serious offence it was and that being accused would mean they would never ever play for India. I was also a little scared that by raising this sensitive episode constantly I might make them all the more conscious. So I just told the team to put everything behind them and focus on winning matches for the country.

My captaincy model was characterized by two distinctive pillars. Proper identification of talent and then ensuring the young finds played fearless cricket. The toughest challenge for an Indian captain was to keep track of talented domestic players as he was touring most of the time. I had to delegate the responsibility to one or two selectors I trusted almost blindly. My policy was simple. East, west, north or south didn't matter. What mattered was the player's personal skill. I wanted complete honesty in team selection. I was a firm believer in attitude. I always thought good attitude was infectious. Once I picked a player I supported him all the way.

The senior members were as important and I never

neglected them. I wanted leaders in different groups. Be it batting, bowling or fielding. I also created a core group in the team. Apart from me and Rahul, this included Sachin, Anil and Srinath. The team was not just mine but theirs as well.

They were like a crack team working along with the captain. All of them were capable of leading India – I believed it was only incidental that I was leading. We were a close-knit group; not once was I made to feel insecure. There are captains who have stayed away from discussions and run the team autocratically. I have seen captains getting defensive when others have made well-meaning suggestions. I have never led like that.

We quickly blooded youngsters like Zaheer, Yuvraj and Harbhajan. Sehwag came a little later. The biggest challenge was to ensure that they would perform up to their potential and win matches for India. I believed that the energy of the players should focus entirely on winning matches for India rather than playing safe. They should never think negatively – what will happen if I fail?

Many of these decisions were coloured by what I had seen in the early part of my career. The message was clear – I shall back you even if you fail. In return I expect you to play no-holds-barred cricket.

When I asked Sehwag to open in Test cricket, he was understandably nervous. He told me quite anxiously, 'Agar main fail ho jayen toh?' I assured him, Viru, irrespective of what happens, you will remain in the side.

The reason I promoted Viru was that I realized Australia was beginning to change the landscape of Test match batting with Hayden and Langer. I thought we needed to fire from the top as well to catch up with the trend. Even after succeeding as an opener Viru made statements in the press that he was more comfortable in the middle order. I ignored that. To this day I firmly believe Viru would have been half the batsman if he had stayed in the middle order.

Picking Harbhajan Singh was another gamble. I remember in the very first year of my captaincy I was told by one of the selectors to have a look at this young spinner from Punjab. I had not seen him bowl till then. So I requested the BCCI to fly him down to where we were playing. I left it to Kumble to decide Bhajji's future.

As a captain, I had over the years constantly looked out for players who remain steady under pressure and possess the capability to change the course of the match. Mahendra Singh Dhoni, who came to my notice in 2004, was a natural progression of this thought.

I was impressed with Dhoni from day one. He was in my team for the Challenger Trophy. After seeing his big hits at the nets, I sent him to open the innings. I have never forgotten his hurricane knock in which he not only got a hundred but tonked Ashish Nehra out of Wankhede Stadium.

Even though the first three batting slots – of Sachin, Sehwag and me – were well settled in my one-day team, we needed one more power hitter so that we could play with seven batters. I felt Dhoni could turn out to be the match-winner we were looking for. Today I am happy that my assessment was proven right. It is amazing how he broke through the ranks to become what he is today. I wish I'd had Dhoni in my 2003 World Cup team. I was told that when we were playing the 2003 World Cup final he was still a ticket collector with Indian Railways. Unbelievable!

John and I had our first joint examination at the Champions Trophy in Nairobi in October that year. We began with a bang, defeating what was then the strongest cricket unit on this earth – Australia. My youngsters didn't disappoint. Eventually we lost in the finals – it was a match we should have won.

Yuvraj Singh had made his debut here and impressed the cricketing world right away. People say how difficult it was to manage Yuvi and all that. Nonsense. For me, handling him was never a problem. Yes, he would meet his friends and have parties. But that didn't matter as he won you matches like the very first one-day in Nairobi.

The next Champions Trophy was played in Colombo. One day a correspondent told me how Wasim Akram had complimented this new-look Indian team. Akram saw us turn the England match away from the brink of defeat. Kaif and I both got hundreds in the match and we survived a knock-out scare. My team reminded Akram of the legendary Pakistan team of the 1980s, where the dressing room didn't believe they could lose. That is why they came back from death on multiple occasions.

For me the praise couldn't have got any bigger.

9

Waving the Shirt at Lord's

Steve Waugh produced an alarm clock out of nowhere.

'I will first go up on the stage holding the clock and tell the audience, look, I have come all the way from Sydney and reached on time. Sourav is only coming from Behala. Yet he keeps me waiting,' he said with a wicked grin.

I quickly said, no Steve, that was gamesmanship – don't take it to heart. This was at a recent cricket talk at the ITC Sonar, Kolkata. While Kapil Dev's partner was the irresistible Viv Richards, I was paired with the most competitive and fearsome captain of my generation.

At night on my way back home I chuckled to myself quietly. It might now be all fun and music but Steve's banter clearly showed that the toss issue had got under his skin. By making him wait at the pitch, I must have caused some irritation for the Aussie captain. Otherwise he would not have mentioned the toss incident a good ten years later.

I must say that I have the greatest respect and admiration for Steve. To me, he remains the ultimate opponent. The captain I most wanted to defeat. I was very surprised when Warne later criticized him for being 'the most selfish cricketer' he had played with. For me Stephen Waugh was and will always remain a visionary. A leader of men.

Yes, we did have our battles and our share of disagreements. One still remains unresolved. He claims I kept him waiting for the toss as many as seven times. I say, no, I was late only three times. He says, me forgetting the blazer in our dressing room was an excuse. I say no. The first time, I really did forget my blazer. Then when I saw it was irritating him, I decided to rub it in.

I have talked about personal comebacks in this book. Well, that 2001 series against Waugh was a huge team comeback and a milestone for me as captain. Before the series I had sat down with coach John Wright to prepare the blueprint for the battle royal.

The Aussie team, then undisputedly the best in the world, had an amazing success rate. They had won 15 consecutive Test matches. At home, spin clearly was the best weapon to stop this juggernaut. But we had a major casualty in that department.

The iconic Kumble had got injured and was preparing for a shoulder operation. This was a massive blow as Kumble contributed not only with his wicket-taking ability but also with a highly inspiring presence in the dressing room. Little did I know that Bhajji would perform with so much fire that even the great Kumble's absence would hardly be felt.

We had made an extensive game plan for all the players, highlighting their strengths and weaknesses as part of our team dossier. But our loss in the first Test in Mumbai and the way in which the Australians applied gamesmanship on the field forced me to look for an alternative. I knew I had to think out of the box.

It didn't help that the Aussies were master sledgers, whose bluster was designed to hit where it hurt most. After that highly disappointing first Test, I decided to play the Board President's game against Australia in Delhi. On day three of the match I had to leave before the scheduled close of play as the board's travel agency had given me a 6.30 p.m. flight for Kolkata. Steve saw me coming off the ground and said, 'A captain who sits out half the time without battling it out on the field with his players – how is he going to inspire the team?'

Mark Waugh in Mumbai had also continuously sledged us from the slips. He said to the batsmen, 'Hey, you are gone guys. If you have prepared a turner we have a Warne. For a grassy pitch we have McGrath. Where will you hide?' I was repeatedly taunted by the Aussie close-in fielders that I would be sacked after this series defeat.

I decided enough was enough. We would have to hit back. And we did in the next Test at Eden Gardens, which has gone down as arguably the greatest Test match played in India. A freak Test for me. It was the first time the Aussies were stopped in their tracks after a long winning streak.

My two weapons were Harbhajan and Laxman.

Of all the knocks I have seen in my cricketing career, Laxman's 281 tops the list. I have never seen anyone hit Warne continuously against the turn through midwicket so effortlessly. In the 34 overs that Warne bowled in that innings he gave away 153 runs and could take only one wicket. Unbelievable.

I would rank the best knocks I have seen from Indian batsmen in this order

1. Laxman's 281 at Kolkata
2. Sachin's 114 at Perth
3. Sehwag's 309 at Multan
4. Rahul's 148 at Headingley
5. Kohli's second innings hundred at Adelaide

Laxman today is one of my best friends. He is artistry and grace personified even off the field and never buckles under pressure. Laxman's partner in Eden was Rahul. Together they had scored a superb 376. Two years later, Rahul would partner Laxman in Adelaide for another huge triple-century partnership. I had so much faith in these two that I didn't send out a single message while they were batting. I just sat in the dressing room and kept on praying.

We had beaten Australia at home and played some truly extraordinary cricket. But I knew what counted was winning overseas. Wherever India went, be it South Africa, Australia, New Zealand, we had the same model. We kept on playing spinners and our opponents gleefully ensured there wasn't even a single dry patch on the pitch. It made our one-dimensional attack completely ineffective.

The day I became captain I told myself this age-old policy had to change. Enough of romance. We needed to get real. I wanted to build a bank of fit and strong fast bowlers and create a new template. I said, within the subcontinent, the emphasis will be on spinners. But outside, pacers will have to assume primary responsibility for picking 20 wickets.

I was fortunate enough to have Srinath in the side. The rest of the pacers were good but certainly not match-winners. I discussed this with the selectors and said, please look for someone who bowls with a bit of zip. If you find someone like that, don't keep him in domestic cricket. Pick him straight away for India. This is why Zaheer Khan played so few domestic matches before the selectors picked him for the Champions Trophy in Nairobi. And suddenly he found himself standing with the new ball against the mighty Adam Gilchrist.

I believed in throwing the younger players at the deep end. The better ones did handle themselves, swam their way and beat the odds. Bhajji for instance. The selectors wanted to drop him after the Mumbai Test against Australia. They wanted to play Sarandeep Singh. But I resisted. I had seen a spark in Harbhajan and he justified my faith by almost single-handedly winning us the series.

Then at the South Africa tour selection, the North Zone selector did not want to pick Sehwag. He felt Sehwag would find it difficult to score on those pacy, bouncy pitches of South Africa. But I backed Viru and was proven right.

Incidentally, my first Test as the Indian captain happened to be Bangladesh's maiden Test match. Now the cricket craze in Bangladesh is almost unparalleled. I always got a lot of affection there. It was almost as if I was playing for them. Sheikh Hasina, the prime minister of Bangladesh, has always been extremely affectionate. I also have many friends in that country.

Among the cricketers there are quite a few. Mashrafe Mortaza, Akram Khan, Habibul Bashar, Anamul Haque. But I would mostly spend time with the Bangladeshi cricket officials. Someone like Mithu bhai, a businessman in Dhaka, who I knew from my Under 19 days. The best thing about Mithu was that he never talked shop after the day's play. He became like extended family. There were others like Tito, Ashrafulda and Babu bhai. Other attractions include a restaurant in Gulshan which serves exquisite Thai food plus the hilsa and the jamdani saris that I bought there.

However, on the ground it was cricket at its hardest. Serious cricket onlookers took note of my shift in strategy when I played three pace bowlers in Dhaka. It was unheard of that an Indian team playing in the subcontinent would play two spinners and three pacers. I was criticized. But it didn't stop me. My take on criticism is simple – if your job attracts attention you are bound to get evaluated. Some will offer bouquets. Some may throw brickbats. You have to learn to live with both.

The real turnaround in our overseas strategic thinking happened in the West Indies at the Trinidad Test match. I saw the pitch in the morning and decided to leave out Kumble. I went in with a 3+1 combination. Playing Bhajji and leaving Kumble was a huge decision. I had picked an extra pace bowler in Nehra. Every time I kept Kumble out, the champion bowler would look at me with an astounded face, as if I was making a huge mistake. Eventually, we won the Trinidad Test. My decision was vindicated as Nehra bowled superbly in the match.

I decided to do away with the age-old beliefs of the touring Indian team. I strongly believed if the mindset was right any situation could be handled. My decision to bat at the Headingley test in 2002 after winning the toss has to be viewed in this context. It was perplexing to the onlookers that an Indian captain had won the toss and chosen to bat on that green pitch.

Ian Botham questioned me at the toss. He was most surprised when he heard that we were batting. I intentionally did the opposite of what was expected as I wanted our batting line-up to soak in the pressure and we played two spinners and five bowlers in all on that pitch. We ended up winning the Test by an innings. Kumble later remarked it was our defining victory of that era as it showed that India could win in adverse overseas conditions.

Also along with the coach we managed to create an atmosphere where match-winners were rewarded, irrespective of their age and experience. Quite a few youngsters had come up. The likes of Yuvraj, Kaif, Sehwag, Parthiv. To motivate them further I changed my on-field personality.

Off the field I was docile, introverted, a little withdrawn. Now I became aggressive on the field. I learned this tactic in the famous Eden Gardens Test in 2001. It was a tense game and I noticed that quite a few of our players were reacting aggressively to the pressure tactics of the Australians. They were giving it back.

This was not planned. It happened spontaneously. But

I decided to use the same approach in the future. I would pick up a fight with the opponent just to get Harbhajan or Zaheer fired up. Our coach successfully tried the same trick on me.

Before the legendary NatWest final, I had a disagreement with John and we were not talking. Once we won the match and started celebrating I noticed an arm tapping my shoulder. I turned around and saw the coach, who smilingly said that this was his idea to pump me up for the big final. I had scored 60 in the match from just 43 balls. John was very good and without his guidance I may not have achieved what I was aspiring to do as a leader.

Though my team had performed very well overseas, one disappointment remained in not winning a Test series in Sri Lanka. The Sri Lankans of course were a top side in those days but we ran them close and lost the 2001 series 1-2. The only Test we won was in Kandy because of my innings of 98 not out and Rahul's solid knock of 65. I had to hear caustic remarks from some experts for not being able to get past Sri Lanka. But the critics conveniently forgot this was a side without Sachin, Srinath, Kumble and Laxman.

On the whole though, it was my great pride to see that the unit had become so resilient. I particularly remember a meeting in Australia where the players were discussing the security risks of the forthcoming Pakistan tour and wondering if it would be safe to go there.

Quite a few said it would be very risky and that we must express our unavailability to the board in writing. They wanted a draft to be prepared at the meeting. But six or seven players put their hands up and said we must go and avail of this opportunity to beat Pakistan in Pakistan, which had never happened before. I felt so proud.

During my captaincy years one incident stood out for its unpleasantness. It was a grossly unfair decision of the former English captain Mike Denness. He was the ICC match referee in South Africa and had suspended six of us after the Bloemfontein Test. Denness had accused Sachin, of all people, of ball-tampering. It was a ridiculous decision.

I had given Sachin the new ball to send down a few overs. He was just polishing the ball and the match referee accused him of ball-tampering. We tried to explain that the ball was still new. Why would anyone tamper with it? But he wouldn't listen. I had to stand up against the referee's decision as a leader. The board had also backed us and what followed was a huge international cricket crisis. But it was refreshing to see the entire team united.

Ian Chappell once told me that when you go to bed at night you must be absolutely sure from the bottom of your heart that you have been honest and treated every player on his own merit. That you selected every player because you felt he was good enough and deserved a place. In the process you might make a few mistakes. It does not matter. It has happened to every captain in history. It will happen in the future also. He said that there are captains who will compromise and there are some who will not. The second type last longer.

My five-year experience suggests captaincy is an amazing disease. It either cures you or kills you. I have seen captains turn into different individuals once they are offered the job.

I have seen personalities of captains change completely as soon as they are at the helm. It also brings unbelievable amount of pressure. Look at Dhoni – he turned grey. Look at me – I lost so much hair.

Everyone has his own way of coping with stress. Mine was music. Like quite a few Indian players I used to carry my own music system on the tour and had an impressive collection of retro songs – from Kishore Kumar to Kumar Sanu. From Asha Bhosle to Abhijeet. From Sonu Nigam to Shaan. Lata Mangeshkar remains a favourite. I have a soft spot for her and could never say no to any request she made of me.

I see a lot of leadership spark in the current Indian captain. I have admired the way Virat Kohli grooms the team members, protects and fights for them. The other day someone told me that he was trying to negotiate with the board to ensure someone like Pujara, who only plays Test cricket, does not suffer financially. For me such instances are the hallmark of a leader.

Apart from Steve, one rival captain I greatly admired was Nasser Hussain. Sachin also had a lot of praise for Nasser. His strategy for playing India in India was highly innovative. Nasser felt that to do well in India he needed to keep the Indian crowd quiet. He feared that if the crowd was happy with the run feast they were watching, the cacophony would be a bit too much for the touring bowlers to handle.

Nasser observed that in the past touring bowlers from his country had lost the plot by bowling too aggressively to the Indian batsmen. So he planned out a defensive bowling strategy for the tour. And a field placement to match the bowling. His model was simple. Don't attack too much. The focus should be to ensure that you don't leak runs and slowly try to suffocate the batsmen. I thought Australia followed the Nasser model successfully in India in 2004.

At the Aaj Tak cricket conclave in London in 2017 Nasser said in his speech, Sourav, in you I saw a captain who wanted to take Indian cricket to a different level and someone who deeply cared for his team. I was flattered and touched to hear a fellow captain say that.

During our playing career, however, we often clashed. At the NatWest final he had said something to Kaif that made the team very angry. The choicest expletives were hurled at him while he came out to bat in our subsequent meeting at the Champions Trophy in Colombo. He was consumed by Nehra after having scored only 1. They scored 269, which in 2002 wasn't a bad target. When Sehwag and I came out to bat, Nasser started his brand of sledging. He said, let us see how you get there. Well, we got there easily with both of us getting hundreds.

After the match Nasser came into my room and was extremely cordial. I signed a shirt for him. While taking the shirt he said, I will never forget the time you took off your shirt at Lord's. It gave me goosebumps to hear that the English captain had silently applauded his Indian counterpart for taking off his shirt at the hallowed Lord's balcony. Wow!

I have never lived down taking off my shirt in Lord's in 2002. It was my way of giving back to Andrew Flintoff. After the series victory in Mumbai earlier that year, Flintoff had taken off his shirt to ridicule us. Our jousting continued through the Test series prior to NatWest. After winning the final in Lord's, I thought I needed to have my say as well.

In some interviews I was asked what I was telling Flintoff while taking off my shirt. Did I abuse him? Threaten him? I broke into a grin and said, oh no. I was only saying Mera Bharat Mahan.

10

Seven Days with Greg Chappell

'So, are you seeing a bit of nightlife in Australia?' Greg Chappell enquired with twinkling eyes and a smile.

I had been training under his watchful eye at the SCG for the last few days. We had a fixed routine – he would pick me up at half past nine sharp from my hotel. Both of us would then drive down to the picturesque SCG for a round of morning practice. But after a few days, I requested him to meet me directly at the ground around half past ten.

'Greg, don't worry,' I said, 'I shall reach on my own.' That's when Greg began to tease me about my late night partying.

Now as you know I am a complete teetotaller. The big city nightlife had never drawn me, unlike some of my more flamboyant colleagues. My reason for delaying our session was for something far less exciting. I wanted to start training on my own before I met with Greg – this involved running thirteen to fourteen laps by the time he got to the grounds. Extensive running was an integral part of my new fitness routine. As the captain I aspired to raise the bar. I knew that especially on a tour as difficult as Australia I had to set the standard.

Sometimes in life you come to a standstill. You might reach a point in your career when things begin to plateau. What does one do next? Do I stop here, accepting this is a dead end? Or do I take a risk and kick-start things once again? There is another, deeper question that lies at the heart of this dilemma, a question about how you want to live your life – should I play safe and just carry on? Or do I have a responsibility to leave behind a legacy?

In the middle of 2003 I encountered a similar dilemma. As a leader I had a successful run in the World Cup, taking the team to the finals before losing to our nemesis, Australia. Before that the team under me had recorded the exciting NatWest trophy win where we beat a strong England team in their home territory. India was also the joint winner in the Champions Trophy. All these were under my belt. But the question was, should I remain content with whatever we had achieved? Or should I as the captain take a fresh, adventurous stance to fly higher?

Our international schedule of the season presented me with an opportunity. We were touring Australia at the end of the year. It was virtually impossible to beat the current team on their home ground. Certainly we had never managed it. Should I, instead of playing safe as a touring captain, decide to attack Australia head-on in their own den? This was one of the finest Australian teams of all time. But that only made the challenge more exhilarating.

When you want to chart a new course you will invariably find people who care for you to be the biggest deterrent. They will always ask you to take the safer route. But as I said earlier, in life safer options will never make you a hero.

You have to take chances. You have to be prepared to lose everything that you have gained. To conquer and create history you have to be always prepared to go beyond the beyond. You might stretch yourself to your absolute limits. You may feel terribly exhausted. Onlookers may declare that you have lost. But if you feel the hunger strongly within, don't ever stop. Go for it. As they say, keep the fire burning! The battle can do wonders, as I experienced while fighting emperor Stephen Waugh in his own palace.

In what would later be viewed as the most defining decision of the series, I decided to go to Sydney in July to do a personal recce before the Test began in December. I thought it would be doubly beneficial. I would use the trip to take my batting to the next level. And it would help me learn more about the playing conditions there.

My team was already motivated to do well down under. But I needed to give their ambitions another push. A little something extra. Sometimes as a leader it's important to make your team see something which might surprise them.

I had less than six months to prepare the team for an examination in what my friend Steve may have termed as the Final Frontier. Attempting to take on Australia in Australia was perhaps more than an adventure. But I dared to dream. Have you seen a skydiver at work? You must have wondered as you watch them fly impossibly in the sky, what will happen if the parachute doesn't open in time? But do the great ones think about it? No, they don't. They just believe they will sail down. Yes, you have to prepare to achieve such confidence. Prepare to succeed. And I was touring Australia to prepare myself and my team to succeed.

I would go early and stand in the middle of the pitch. Set my angles right in the slip gully cordon. I would imagine Zaheer Khan forcing a Mathew Hayden edge to the slip cordon and Laxman or Dravid on duty gladly accepting. Were they standing at the right distance from the batsman? I would stand and measure. Precision is very important here. I didn't want the slip fielders to jump in the air for a delivery which just went past them. Or an edge which fell short as they were standing too far behind. I imagined Dravid accepting a catch at first slip and India celebrating the scorecard. Australia 40-3.

What also affected us in the past were the long Australian boundaries. In the subcontinent we are not used to it. The boundaries are so deep that direct throws were almost out of the question. I had witnessed how our fielders struggled with them on my first trip in 1992. It also affected your batting as quite often you had to run to chalk up 3 runs. That left you too exhausted to face the next delivery. I did my laps at the SCG, and told myself, the big boundaries don't matter. We would conquer them.

I thought Greg Chappell would be the best person to help me. In our previous meetings he had impressed me with his deep cricketing knowledge. Little did I know then that this association was going to be one of the most controversial of that era.

I got Greg's number from a journalist friend. I told Greg if he agreed I could fly down to either Melbourne or Sydney based on his convenience. But I wanted a clear seven days with him.

He was kind enough to accept. The conversation finished quickly and soon I was all ready to board the flight. None of my team members knew I was boarding a flight for Australia. Nor did the press have a clue. I had to, however, inform our board president Jagmohan Dalmiya to officially get clearance. I told him this was necessary to take our team to the next level. But I didn't disclose my real intentions to him – that I would be doing an exhaustive recce of the grounds.

When I reached Australia it was near freezing in Sydney. Greg had cautioned me beforehand that the practice pitches would be a bit damp. I had no problems. I was looking forward to training in the toughest of conditions.

We practised in two sessions with a lunch break in between. Lunch was simple, roast beef sandwich beneath the SCG stands. I picked Greg's brains non-stop about different conditions and situations. I had so many questions.

What was the length at which the bowler is expected to bowl on hard Australian pitches? Which are the toughest conditions in a day's play? On which Australian ground should I play two spinners? What would be the ideal bowling combination for the Gabba? Which side of the ground do I bowl spinners? How do I place the field in a rectangular ground like Adelaide?

We had often been thrashed here because our fielders hadn't been placed accurately and had missed catches. Easy wins that we had dropped.

I had immense respect for Greg's cricketing acumen and I took him to various parts of the ground to get my angles and field placements right. The series was beginning in Brisbane. I requested him to take me to Brisbane for a day. Unfortunately that didn't happen as it was very cold in Brisbane and the ground remained covered with frost.

I went through various batting drills as well. My balance while playing a drive, the ideal body position while effecting a pull, my shot selection, my back foot defence. Everything was discussed in detail.

I returned home after seven days. The Greg Chappell I would see later in my career was completely different from this man. This Greg had made an enormous difference to my game. Before leaving, I thanked him profusely, from the bottom of my heart. I returned completely rejuvenated, and scored a hundred against New Zealand in Ahmedabad.

I also felt immensely happy that I had prepared so well for the Australians. Some of you may find it strange that the captain of a team went to another country for a bit of cricket espionage. But I saw perfect sense in this. I didn't want to show up in December and deal with surprises and unforeseen situations. I even checked into the same hotel where we would stay during the tour.

I later read that John Wright was not aware of my secret Australia tour and apparently it didn't please him. This is anything but true. Wright was fully aware and he knew what I was trying to achieve. He had told me, as a captain you are free to do what you want to do. So he had let me go and see the pitches for myself.

What Australia very cleverly did over the years was to expose the visiting teams early on the tour to the most trying conditions. By the time the visitors got used to the conditions, the series was over. I knew despite planning exhaustively for the series, there would still be tremors. The idea was to minimize their impact to the greatest possible extent.

It used to be said in Indian cricket circles those days that if I ever had the smallest problem, I'd pick up the phone, dial 033, the Kolkata code, and get through to the hotline to reach Jagmohan Dalmiya. The story amused me. I would call Mr Dalmiya only if the matter was very urgent. And that too to protect the interests of the team.

That August I did call, requesting him to give us three clear weeks ahead of the first Test in Australia. The tour itinerary had already been announced by Cricket Australia. They have always been very smart that way. I wanted Mr Dalmiya to use his good offices to ensure that we got some side games at least before the first Test. He pursued the Australian board successfully to organize this for us.

We landed in Australia. Played the first warm-up match in Melbourne against Victoria and then played two more such games in Brisbane. It was a long three-month tour. But the first two weeks I knew would be the toughest. Once we got through that, things would be much easier. And that's exactly what happened. By the time the Brisbane Test began, we'd had twenty sessions of solid practice on those hard pitches. We were ready for Australia.

We had a hugely successful tour. It was arguably the all-time best Test series for an Indian team in that country. On the last day of the Test series, the host team escaped defeat by the skin of their teeth. One determined Steve Waugh stood between our win and a draw in his final Test innings.

What still rings in my ears is the huge applause that I got when I was going to address the press conference after the last Test. The Indian team had truly won the respect of the Australian media and the crowd. No visiting team had challenged them in the last ten years as much as we had.

This was a series which will always remain very close to my heart. For me it was not just a cricketing triumph. It confirmed to me my instincts that however difficult a challenge was you could always aspire to aim high. As I have said earlier, your near and dear ones will ask you to step back. Your predecessors never achieved this, you will wonder, so why risk failure? One part of you will want to pull back. But remember, your decision will define you. Will define your life.

The first Test in Brisbane was good for us. But it was a crucial Test and set the tempo for the rest of the series. It conveyed to Australia in no uncertain terms that we weren't going to be pushovers. We had the first innings lead and my hundred was proof to myself that my hard work had paid off. I knew we had to make a statement early on, or else it would have been a rapid slide downwards.

Dravid caught me in the lobby at the Sheraton after the first Test and asked me how I got the hundred. What homework had I done? I did not reveal much. Just said I had set the platform for my team. That if I could get a hundred at the Gabba, the rest of the team could also score anywhere in the Tasman Sea.

Dravid had scored 1 and 43 not out in Brisbane but had not looked back since. He performed exceptionally well in the series. With his success, I knew the leader in me succeeded. On this tour, Harbhajan, who was nursing an injury, was missing. But Kumble made up for it by his lion-hearted bowling. And of course the much underestimated Ajit Agarkar, who in the second innings of the Adelaide Test demolished the Australian batting.

The Australians, as a part of their well-planned strategy, always targeted the rival captain. I had made up my mind even before fastening the seat belts on the flight that I was going to attack before they realized what had hit them. I rehearsed in my mind the shots that I would employ in those conditions. I had to show it to the team that when the crunch moment arrived the general would not hide behind the bushes. He would lead his troops from the front.

In Brisbane, we were in a commanding position. The Australians were so used to killing opponents in the first Test of the series that they were a little taken aback by us counter-attacking. I could see that in their body language while I raced towards my first Test hundred on Australian soil. While I was going strong Australia tried almost everything in – and outside – the book to stop me.

They would constantly sledge me. I remember Mathew Hayden calling out from the slips, hey, aren't you ashamed that you are leading a team which has Sachin Tendulkar? How can you be his captain? Steve Waugh of course was at it constantly.

I remember once at Eden Gardens when I took a stance in the second innings I saw a truly unusual field setting for me. They had eight fielders on the off side with a lone midwicket patrolling the on side. When I was surveying the field placements with complete disbelief, Steve came up to me and said, son, you have six months left in international cricket. Now enjoy.

I repaid him when he got out to Bhajji in the second innings by saying, hey Steve, after this defeat let me know how you feel. Do you understand you will no longer remain the captain of Australia? It was only friendly banter. He did not say anything. Just walked off. I knew I was fighting a champion and refused to let him get the better of me mentally.

I loved those friendly banters with the Australians. When we toured Australia, Steve was playing his last Test series. Emotions were high. Steve was not just a captain but a national hero. They would all come to the stadium waving the red handkerchiefs which was a trademark of Waugh. The moment he stepped on to the field, a huge cheer would go up. Steve too wanted to finish his career on a high note by dispatching us to the cleaners.

But we were in no mood to remain bystanders at his party. We wanted to spoil his big moment. We went 1-0 up in Adelaide where Rahul Dravid, in both innings of the Test, batted superbly. So did VVS.

A Kolkata-based reporter asked me, Dravid had said a few years ago that when it came to playing the off side, there was god and next was Ganguly. Now what will you say about Dravid's batting here? I replied he was batting like god.

Australia came back strongly by levelling the series at Melbourne. But we didn't surrender meekly. In fact at one point, the fate of the Test hung in the balance. It could have gone either way. We just failed to capitalize on Sehwag's sensational first innings knock and lost the last six wickets for only 16 runs.

The mighty Tendulkar was still not getting runs. His confidence had suffered a bit as well. So in the second innings, towards the end of the day's play, I came in at number 4. During the innings, I got hit by a Brett Lee delivery on the head. It was so heavy a blow that it broke my helmet. I could have changed my helmet instantly and got some medical attention. The back of my head was throbbing in pain. But I decided not to touch the area. I didn't want to give Brett Lee the psychological advantage of enjoying a quiet laugh.

When you played Waugh's invincible Australian team, the mantra was very simple. You were not fighting a battle with them, you were participating in a full-fledged war. You couldn't afford to display the slightest amount of mental weakness. They were so good in using opportunities. I realized that if I slipped up, my team would be psychologically beaten.

In Sydney, during the last Test match of the series Tendulkar returned to form. He then went on to produce a masterclass which will be talked of for generations to come. His massive double hundred and the marathon partnership with VVS left the Aussie crowd on tenterhooks.

We consolidated Sachin's superb batting with a bowling attack which had the Aussies reeling. It was supremely satisfying to see the mighty Australian side fighting for survival on their own turf. When Steve came out to bat in the second innings we all stood back and gave him a guard of honour. But we didn't slack either.

Parthiv Patel behind the stumps was the most active of all. The close-in fielders were part of the game plan too. Even a hardened pro like Steve lost his cool, and got into an argument with the stockily built wicketkeeper. But being the champion that he was, he succeeded in taking Australia to safety once again.

We stayed back in the country to continue with the one-day series. My job, however, was mostly done.

Back home in 2004 while we were discussing who could succeed John Wright, his name flashed in my mind first. I thought Greg Chappell would be the best person to take us to the number one slot from the challenger's position. I had conveyed my personal choice to Mr Dalmiya when they were looking for a new Indian coach.

A few people advised me against this move. Sunil Gavaskar was one of them. Sourav, think about it. With him around you might have problems in running the team. His past coaching record is not spectacular, he told me.

Mr Dalmiya also called one morning and asked me to come to his house for an urgent discussion. He shared in confidence that even his brother Ian thought Greg might not be the right choice for India. I had no reason to disbelieve this as Mr Dalmiya was quite friendly with Ian Chappell.

Well, I decided to ignore all these warnings and follow my instincts. The rest as they say is history. But then that's life. Some scripts go your way, like my tour of Australia, and some don't, like the Greg chapter. I conquered the country but not one of its citizens.

11

Handling Pakistan

I have toured Pakistan quite a number of times but the security that was laid out for us in 2004 was the tightest I had ever witnessed. I always thought the Sri Lankans gave us the maximum security because of the Liberation Tigers of Tamil Eelam. But the famous Pearl Continental Hotel in Lahore where we checked in felt like a fortress.

And can you believe it, I, the Indian captain, escaped one day from the fortress well past midnight for a bit of adventure with my friends. I knew it was breaking the rules, that I was violating the security code, but I felt I had to get away from the rifles and tanks.

We had won the historic one-day series in Pakistan, the first time Pakistan had lost a series against us on their own soil. I was badly injured on the field while attempting a catch and after the match was asked by the doctor to rest for three weeks. But that night I was in such a cheerful mood that I didn't quite understand the seriousness of the injury.

Some of my dear friends had come from Kolkata to watch the series decider. I was extremely happy seeing them. The satisfaction was immense as we had trailed 1-2 in the series and then recorded back-to-back victories. The margin in the last match was 40 runs but it hardly demonstrated the closeness of the match which could have gone either way.

Well past midnight I discovered that my friends were making plans to visit the iconic Food Street for kebabs and exotic tandoori dishes. The area is famously known as Gawalmandi. It is one of the most famous food streets of the subcontinent.

By then the security was getting to me and I was longing for freedom. When I spotted the Kolkata gang, including the co-writer of this book, in the lobby, I immediately decided to go along. I didn't dare inform our security officer as I knew he would have stopped me from going. I had only told our team manager Ratnakar Shetty that I was going out with a couple of friends. I quietly slipped through the back door armed with a cap which covered half my face. Even my teammates did not know that I had gone out with absolutely no security.

Now the Food Street was an open space where you always ran the danger of getting recognized. I had devised my own formula to counter such threats.

'Arey aap Sourav Ganguly ho na?' someone asked excitedly.

I said no in a slightly modulated voice. He shook his head and said, 'I thought as much. Par aap bilkul Sourav jaise dikhte ho.'

My friends and I tried hard to control our laughter as another man appeared from nowhere and said, 'Sir, aap idhar? Kya badhiya khela aap ki team.' I completely ignored him and behaved as if I had nothing to do with cricket. This man also shook his head and walked away.

My friends admitted that I was doing a great job at keeping the fans at bay. We were about to finish our dinner when someone finally called my bluff. A few yards from where we sat on those old-fashioned steel chairs, I was spotted by the journalist Rajdeep Sardesai. He was having dinner with the then Indian minister for information and broadcasting Ravi Shankar Prasad. The moment Rajdeep spotted me, he started shouting, Sourav, Sourav.

I knew I was in trouble. The minister's security meanwhile arrived to escort me to his table. Within a few minutes the news spread like wildfire that the Indian captain was in Food Street. People started coming in from all directions and I got gheraoed.

I was finishing the last bits of the delicious kebabs and didn't realize the situation would turn out of control so quickly. While I tried to pay the bill and escape from there the shopkeeper refused to accept payment. He kept on saying, 'Bahut achcha. We need someone as aggressive as you to lead Pakistan.'

By then my friends were beginning to get worried, as the crowds had grown. A few policemen arrived from nowhere and escorted me back to the car. While we were making our way back to the hotel a speeding motorbike chased our car. The biker was asking me to roll down the window. My co-passengers kept telling me not to as they feared he might have a bomb. I, however, did not see any threat and obliged him. He stretched out his hand and echoed the shopkeeper in Food Street, 'I am a big fan of yours. Pakistan needs a leader like you.' The series loss had hurt the average supporter big time.

There were no more incidents and I reached our hotel safely. I was feeling a little guilty but convinced myself that I hadn't done anything intentionally to break the security code. I was just happy after winning the series, I told myself. After all, life on a long tour often gets lonely and at times you need release. I reassured myself that I had managed it well, and that there had been no real damage done. Just the presence of Rajdeep Sardesai had ruined it all; otherwise I would have been able to return undetected. But as they say in the movies, the picture was still not over. What happened next morning was sensational. I shall come to that later.

I loved touring Pakistan. They are also part of the third world like India. Poverty is as much an issue there as in our country. But the elite in that country opened their heart to the Indian cricketers and they knew how to live life and dine in style. In terms of hospitality I felt the Pakistanis were second to none. A Pakistan tour thus invariably presented many memorable moments. Both on and off the field.

The first time I toured that country was in 1997. I went to a salwar kameez shop in Lahore to get a couple of exquisite suits for my wife. When the items were packed and I was about to pay, the man at the counter said, 'We won't accept money from you. This is a small token of love from us.' I tried hard to convince him but the shopkeeper remained unmoved. He kept on saying, 'Aap Indiawale hamare bhai hain.'

On another occasion in 2004, our team manager had taken me to his army friend's house for dinner. Our host happened to be a Pathan. I have never forgotten their affection and the dinner spread that was laid out for us. The

Like all good Bengalis I love the Pujas. Here I am celebrating my favourite festival – once as myself, the other disguised as one of Harbhajan's tribe.

With my daughter Sana – I love her more than the game! And (*top*) with my wife Dona and Sana.

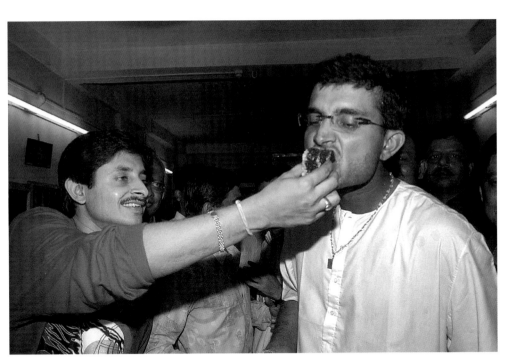

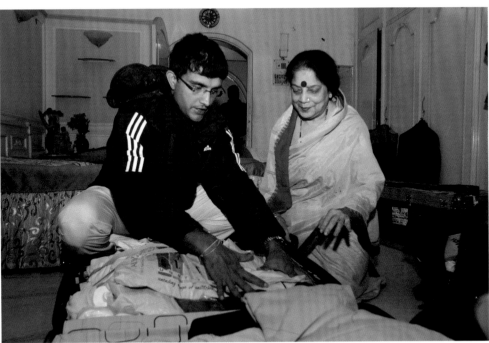

I come from a loving (and sometimes overprotective!) family.
Here is my brother Snehasish feeding me (*top*) and my mother
Nirupa Ganguly helping me pack my kitbag (*bottom*).

Top: I have never forgotten Imran Khan's words to me as a young player.

Bottom: Sunil Gavaskar admiring my hairstyle.

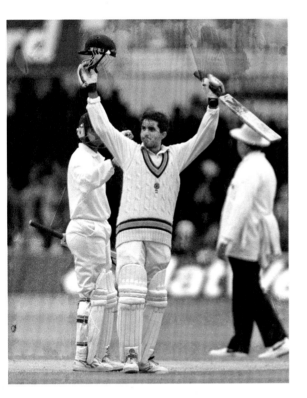

Making my mark. The debut century at Lord's (*top*) – the London ground has been one of my favourites ever since – and in Taunton (*left*) in the 1999 World Cup. My 183 is the highest score by an Indian cricketer in a World Cup till date.

My approach as a captain was simple: identify talent through selection.
And as you can see above the selection sometimes happened on the greens.
Once I had picked the right talent, give them space. The team had to feel
enthused, passionate and secure.

The 2001 win against Australia in Eden: a series that changed the face of Indian cricket.

Top: The picture I could never live down: celebrating the NatWest victory at Lord's, 2002.

Bottom: Crossing bats with Inzamam-ul-Haq: our victory in Pakistan was one of the high points of my captaincy in 2003.

Victorious in Pakistan: the jubilant team in Rawalpindi (*bottom*)
and a private celebration mid-air (*top*).

Top: Victory to Team India: we were the only Indian team to win both the Test and the ODI series in Pakistan.

Bottom: Prime Minister Vajpayee had said, '*Series jeeto aur dil bhi jeeto.*' We did both.

Top: My ultimate test as captain was playing the world's greatest team on their home turf in 2003 and nearly beating them. Here Steve Waugh and I walk for the toss in Melbourne on Boxing Day. Waugh was simply the best.

Bottom: Shoaib Akhtar is the one cricketer who can really make me laugh.

A tale of two coaches. I've always had an excellent equation with John Wright (*left*). Snooker time with a different type of coach (*top*).

Post-Chappell comeback: in South Africa (*bottom left*), winning the
Man of the Series title in the 2007 India–Sri Lanka series (*top*) and
scoring my only century against Pakistan at home in Eden (*bottom right*).

Top: Shah Rukh and me in my final year with KKR.

Bottom: The gesture that turned into a controversy – my action was construed by the press as a challenge to Shah Rukh Khan.

With my fans after the final test.

Me today – on a new journey.

ever charismatic Imran Khan also invited us to his hilltop bungalow, Bani Gala, in Islamabad for dinner. Again, Imran's hospitality was mind-blowing.

For all the fun off the field, playing Pakistan was always a charged affair – not just in Pakistan and India but in all the neutral venues, be it Sharjah, Toronto, Australia, Sri Lanka or South Africa. Every time you played them you noticed something was different. It was always eventful. But during my five-year captaincy career it is the incident at the Centurion in South Africa during the 2003 World Cup that remains one of the highlights for me.

A scuffle had taken place between Harbhajan Singh and Yousuf Youhana in the common lunch arena. I did not know what led to the fight. But the scene was getting out of control and senior members of both the teams had to finally separate them. An Indo-Pak tie was always just that little bit extra tense. So the atmosphere was already heated. It also did not help matters that unlike other South African grounds the dressing rooms of the two teams were too close for comfort.

I spoke to the openers before they went in. Particularly Sehwag. I didn't want him to get affected by this pressure-cooker situation. We were chasing 273 against the likes of Akram, Waqar and Shoaib. We needed a solid opening partnership at any cost. So I cautioned Viru, it is a good batting wicket. Don't take chances early. After 10 overs we will accelerate.

What a joke the captain's instructions turned out to be! India raced to 60 for no loss in 5 overs. Sachin and Sehwag just ripped apart the Pakistani bowling. The hapless

Indian captain, instead of complaining, was smiling ear to ear. I realized this was a huge knockout punch and would motivate us throughout the tournament.

The Centurion dressing room had a small viewing area. By the time the winning stroke was hit the entire team was down there. It was neither the final nor the semi-final yet it was a once-in-a-lifetime atmosphere. Our joy knew no bounds and back home in India the fans had already started celebrating Diwali in March with firecrackers. By the way, I got a call from the Chief of the Army Staff after we beat Pakistan at the Centurion. If I had any doubts about the importance of this match, that call put it in the right perspective.

From my childhood Indo-Pak matches presented nothing less than a carnival. Those early memories of watching the matches were not very bright. Pakistan had one of the all-time great teams under the great Imran Khan and India would lose to them mostly. I remember watching the first one-day match at Eden Gardens where India were on the verge of winning the match when Salim Malik turned it around. The way Malik smashed the legendary Kapil Dev all around the ground was just incredible.

Other than in the World Cups, the Pakistan juggernaut seemed to move easily against India.

I grew up watching epic Sharjah matches and I particularly remember one match where Wasim Akram hit Tendulkar on the helmet. Waqar Younis also seemed impregnable with his deadly reverse swings. The best part about the Pakistani greats lay in their ability to quickly think out of the box and find a solution. Waqar had this amazing ability. Pakistan bowlers of my generation were very street smart. They were also full of self-confidence.

I, too, gained in confidence in my early Test years by beating Pakistan. I first played them in Toronto. Then came my first Pakistan trip in 1997 where we had gone to play the Independence Cup. It was a three-match series where I won the first one for India and narrowly missed a hundred. I decimated Waqar in that game – a performance I feel very pleased about. I am talking about an era when Waqar was at his peak. He had arrogance and aggression written all over him when he walked to the bowling run-up. By hitting him all over the park I was sending a message to the Pakistan team – I was here to stay. My domination in the next Toronto series was even more complete.

Every time India played Pakistan there was intense pressure all around. From the tea boy next door to the Indian president, everyone wanted a win. It was never just another cricket match. My success rate against Pakistan is high because I managed to train my mind and manipulate the surroundings to treat this as just another cricket match.

I understood one thing pretty early. The only way you could save yourself from these impossible external forces was to cut them off. However, there was a little problem. You could cut off the external world but what about the room service boy who brought you dinner? Or the housekeeping in-charge? The man with a smiling face who took out your daily laundry?

Well, I devised a plan for them as well. Every time we played Pakistan, a day before the match I made myself completely unavailable. The room service boy rang the bell and came in but found no one in the room. I would hide in the toilet and ask him to keep the food on the table. I would later sign the bill and keep it outside with the tray. My reason was simple. I didn't want to face him before we played Pakistan. I wanted to remain in my own space in a completely undisturbed state of mind.

I did the same whenever I played a match at Eden Gardens and especially against Pakistan. My only hundred in my home town was against Pakistan. Even though I got runs all around the world, my performance at Eden left a lot to be desired. The problem was that I knew far too many people there. Their well-meaning smiles and endless good wishes created a pressure. Love and warmth made me soft.

Every human being who came in close contact with me now was viewed with suspicion. Comforting smiles and good wishes before the match were a complete no-no. My security guard was included in the list and I avoided direct eye contact with him. I had to be careful of the catering staff who served food at the ground. Many were so warm that they would come to me with the extra fish or some additional biryani. So much love and affection made me weak.

I said to myself, Sourav, enough of this friendly Eden Gardens ambience. Get the hell out of this trap of hospitality. For heaven's sake score some runs in your backyard. We had a masseur named Pintu who incidentally has the strongest hands in the business. After a tough day's play, a session with Pintu was the best way to relax. I decided to disconnect his phone as well. What's worse, I refused to recognize him. When he asked me whether I wanted a session, I said curtly that I didn't. Now Pintu is a very nice guy and he was stunned by my behaviour. But I was unrelenting. I had to do this to succeed.

Mother was the next casualty. I shouted at her before I went out to play Pakistan in 2001. I felt terrible later. My mother had this habit of waking me up at seven in the morning and doing puja for me. She would then escort me to the puja room to offer prayers and complete the ritual by serving me a lavish breakfast.

How will you play Wasim Akram and Shoaib Akhtar in the pre-lunch session if you've had delicious luchi and rasgolla for breakfast? So I told my mother very rudely that when I played in other parts of India or abroad – be it Mohali, Cape Town or Adelaide – I didn't get to see her in the morning, did I? So she should make herself scarce here for me as well. I issued strict instructions that when I left in the morning I didn't wish to see anybody. I said just leave a cup of tea for me on the dining table and disappear.

Records seem to suggest that this model worked for me and very soon I was out of my Eden Gardens blues. In 1999 I had disappointed a sizeable Eden Gardens crowd by not taking them home on the all-important last day. Wasim Akram's masterpiece had consumed me. Thirteen years later I salvaged my pride. Inspired by my hundred, India withstood the Pak pressure and the Eden Test ended in an honourable draw.

I similarly found redemption in another Indo-Pak match in Chinnaswamy. The Indian team led by me had lost the last Test and could not retain the 1-0 lead in the Test series. It finished at 1-1. The cricket-loving Bengaluru crowd was hardly happy and I got booed.

Two years later, I scored a double hundred in the same grounds, against the same opponents. In the second innings I should have got a hundred as well but got out in the nineties. The 2007 series was my last against Pakistan and I did fairly well. In Delhi, my second innings knock of 48 and two vital wickets had swung the match in India's favour and we ended up winning the series.

If you look closely at my overall records against Pakistan, I scored an aggregate of 902 runs, averaging 47.47. In one-dayers it is better. Of the 22 centuries I made in one-day matches, 18 took us to victory, which included two against Pakistan.

During the long years of playing Pakistan I made some friends across the border. Wasim, Waqar, Inzi and of course Shoaib Akthar. My first encounter with Shoaib was at Eden Gardens where he had polished off India's middle order by getting Sachin and Dravid in successive deliveries. I was introduced to him properly a few months later at the Hobart hotel lobby when we were touring Australia.

I had heard that he had written to the Pakistan Cricket Board demanding the same wages as the seniors. As we chatted, I found myself intrigued by this rookie fast bowler who was hardly four or five Test matches old and yet comparing himself to the two Ws who by then had taken more than 700 international wickets! I found the confidence arresting. If he had conducted himself better, he would easily have taken another 100 Test wickets.

No discussion on Shoaib can ever be complete without talking about his accent. I don't know how and where he developed this British-Pakistani English of his. I sometimes found it difficult to understand what he was saying. I have a sneaking suspicion that so did he.

I have one strong memory of Shoaib from the 2004 series. I saw him bowling alone at about eleven at night before the Rawalpindi one-dayer. There was no one else in the ground, but it didn't matter. He bowled for nearly three-quarters of an hour. It was an amusing sight. Shoaib had played in the previous one-dayer at Karachi and gone for 55 in his 10 overs.

I still don't know what he was trying to do that night. Was he sending a message to his team or was he trying to convey something to us? I had a quiet chuckle watching him. In my first press conference, I had joked that we would pull the chain of the Rawalpindi Express. I thought the comment may have put Shoaib under pressure.

Wasim Akram was another Pakistani great I admired. I was very keen on roping him in as the bowling coach of the Indian team. I have not seen a greater magician on a cricketing field. They say he was the Sultan of Swing. I beg to differ. To me, he was the shopping mall of pace bowling. You could get whatever you wanted. Maybe because of the troubled Indo-Pak relations, my attempts to get him as the bowling coach for the Indian team didn't succeed. But for our pacers who needed help he was always just a phone call away.

Once I had taken Zaheer Khan to meet Wasim in Nairobi during the Champions Trophy. In his customary tongue-in-cheek fashion, Wasim asked, 'Do you drink?'

Zaheer said, 'No.'

'Do you smoke?'

Zaheer was talking to a senior so he could only think of the obvious no.

Wasim was not impressed one bit. He thundered, 'How will you be a fast bowler if you do not smoke? If you do not drink.' We burst out laughing. I did manage to get Wasim to advise Irfan Pathan before he played his first Test match in Adelaide. Eventually I managed to rope in Wasim as the bowling consultant of Kolkata Knight Riders.

I missed out playing against the Pakistani legend Javed Miandad. My proper entry into international cricket and his exit after the 1996 World Cup almost coincided. Of course I heard some great Miandad stories from the boys who played him. His banter was legendary.

I remember a hilarious encounter I had with him. We were playing the first match of the one-day series in Karachi. Pakistan were chasing a pretty stiff target of 349 and ran us close. Inzamam hit a brilliant hundred and they eventually folded up at 344. Miandad was their coach. He got so involved with the match that towards the final few overs he appeared on the dressing room balcony from where he shouted instructions to his batsmen.

Inzamam was fighting a lone battle but Moin Khan seemed competent enough to partner him through the dying stages. Miandad kept on shouting from the balcony. He was showing Moin where to hit. Moin had scored a valuable 16 at a stage where every run was worth a fifty. I started following Miandad's hand signals, and began to post my fielders exactly where he was asking Moin to hit. Very soon we had the measure of Moin and eventually the match.

But I was very impressed with Miandad's commitment

and his fighting spirit. During the series I had a few opportunities to talk to him. He was full of humorous one-liners. But what struck me most was that this man still appeared to be batting for Pakistan, he was that committed.

I of course was lucky enough to know their captain very well. Inzy was not just one of their greatest players but also a lovely soul. Looking back, I feel we were fortunate that he was leading Pakistan in 2004 as the spirit between the two teams remained excellent despite the frenzied atmosphere outside.

The Pakistani cricketer I owe the most to is an illustrious colleague of Miandad, Zaheer Abbas. During my comeback trail in 2006 I was a little tentative with my grip and stance. I was not getting enough time to play the fast bowlers. While playing for Northamptonshire I met Zed bhai, as I affectionately called him. He really knew his cricket and gave me invaluable advice.

He made me stand a little more upright. While facing pacers, he told me to be more chest on than side on. My grip also changed automatically. Adjusting to the changed stance was difficult but as time went by I became very comfortable with it and got much more time handling pacers. One of the best phases of my career was to begin a few months from then and when it happened I had Zed bhai to thank for it.

One incident during my Pakistan tour as captain remains notorious in cricketing circles. That was the Dravid declaration in Multan while Sachin was batting at 194. The other day Dravid recently jokingly said that in all these years so many people had asked him, why did you declare, that

159

if he had charged each person one rupee he would have become a multi-millionaire.

I began with my escapade to Gawalmandi. I must also share what happened the next morning. I confessed to the team manager about my night out. I can't say he was very pleased. Confession over, I went back to my room and the phone rang.

The call was from President Musharraf's office. The voice on the phone said the president wanted to speak to me. I was tongue-tied. What had happened to make the Pakistan president call the Indian captain?

President Musharraf was polite but firm. He said, next time you want to go out please inform the security and we will have an entourage with you. But please don't indulge in adventures. I was mortified. Facing Wasim Akram's deadly in-cutter was less scary!

Part Three

Giving Up Is Not an Option

12

Hitting Rock Bottom

This remains the most turbulent chapter of my life. Not only was my captaincy suddenly taken away for no reason but I was also dropped as a player. I feel angry even as I write this. What happened was unthinkable. Unacceptable. Unforgivable.

History hasn't recorded many instances of a winning captain being dropped so unceremoniously, that too after scoring a hundred in the last Test series.

In Indian cricket there are no such parallels and I doubt whether there will ever be. So Mr Gregory Stephen Chappell and the selection committee led by Kiran More have indeed put me in august company.

The day Greg got appointed was 20 May 2005. I still remember speaking on the phone with him, immediately after the board had sent out a release confirming his appointment. He was in Delhi and I was in England and our long-distance call was full of happiness and warmth.

Sri Lanka was his first assignment, followed by Zimbabwe. Sri Lanka was scheduled for end July. County cricket had kept me busy in between and when I returned for the Bengaluru camp I sensed that everything was not

165

right. Within a short period he seemed to have changed completely.

I still don't know how he formed such negative opinions about me without me being present. A Kolkata-based journalist friend once suggested that someone poisoned Greg's mind against me. He was talking about John Wright.

I completely disagree. John has always been like family to me. We have a relationship based on complete trust and belief. I was even close to his children and still remain emotionally connected to him. He was a great support to me during the comeback trail and called often.

After we came back from Zimbabwe, I was suffering from a case of tennis elbow. The injury was diagnosed by the team physio John Gloster and I was advised rest. Our itinerary was planned with a big gap between the last day of the second Test in Harare and the first one-day against Sri Lanka in November. I was sure that this was enough time for my injury to heal.

The board had organized a Challenger Trophy tournament in Chandigarh and marked it as the selection trial. I duly submitted the physio's certificate as the cause for non-participation. Around the same time, I started hearing that all was not right. That certain things were happening behind my back.

The coach's secret email to the board was published in a Bengali daily. It said that I was mentally and physically unfit to lead the team, that the rest of the players had been made to feel 'fearful and distrusting' of me and that it was time for me to move on 'and let someone else build their team toward the 2007 World Cup'.

No coach has ever written about his captain in such a dismissive manner in the history of cricket. The news spread like wildfire and the board had to convene an enquiry committee meeting in Mumbai. Greg and I were both asked to depose before the committee. I presented my own version quite forcefully before the enquiry committee and thought they found it convincing. I never imagined that things would turn for the worse.

Greg suggested after the committee meeting that I should stay back for the night and have a one-on-one with him to thrash out things. I was in no mood to do so. The mail had proven exactly how trustworthy he was.

Of course I knew that he wanted me out of the side. I had a very bitter argument with him in Zimbabwe about this. I knew he was gunning for me. But I also knew that I had solid performance to back me up. The team for the Sri Lanka one-day series was to be picked within the next few days. With the selection around the corner, all sorts of stories were doing the rounds. The entire cricketing fraternity waited in anticipation, waiting for the next instalment of the drama.

Well, Rahul Dravid was named the new captain and a certain Sourav Ganguly who had developed Team India into a fighting outfit was shown the door. A captaincy career that had begun in February 2000 in a spectacular fashion ended with barely a whimper in October 2005.

It had taken me about three years to build a new template for the team, a team with a killer instinct that took pride in winning overseas. They threw that leader straight down the trash. The excuse given was that I did not have match fitness. I was shell-shocked. I couldn't believe that they would drop me from the team. To say it was a travesty of justice would be an understatement.

And what was the fitness issue? I had just scored a hundred before the selection. Just before the one-day team was getting picked, the selection committee had directed me to prove my fitness by participating in a Duleep Trophy match in Rajkot. This was a strange decision which had no recent precedence.

With my enormous experience of playing non-stop international cricket for ten years, it could easily have been avoided. I realized this was only a ploy to delay my return to the team. I did go and participate in the Rajkot game where East Zone was playing North – and got a hundred before lunch, that too on a green top. My critics couldn't have been too happy.

That evening, the team got picked and I was overlooked. I sat alone trying to absorb the news. What was the yardstick for selection, I wondered.

Runs? The scoreboard said it all.

Centuries? Only Sachin had scored more one-day hundreds. But we were almost neck and neck. And I had a hundred in my kitty from the most recent Test series in Zimbabwe.

Fitness? Had they read the physio's report?

Age? I was only thirty-three.

The selection criteria had to be about something other than my batting and runs.

The ex-Indian captain in me also felt sad that the dressing room spirit that he had built would now be a thing of the past. I had built a culture of no fear. A culture which instilled a belief that if you performed no one could touch you.

And even if you failed to perform, your place in the team wouldn't be taken away from you. You would get multiple opportunities. But now that the team had seen that even the strongest in the unit could easily be thrown out, insecurity was bound to creep in.

I was left out for a month and a half and waited eagerly for the next team selection. The media of course couldn't get enough of the story. I was used to getting press attention but I was now under constant scrutiny. Every day my name would appear in the papers. The nature of the headlines changed though. It was no longer how Ganguly could have led better today. But how Guru Greg was blocking Ganguly's entry back into the team.

At one point, I stopped reading the papers. India won the one-day series against Sri Lanka convincingly and I realized my job from now onward would get increasingly difficult as the selection committee headed by Kiran More wouldn't be in a hurry to change the winning combination. India's next assignment was to play South Africa led by Graeme Smith. Speculation grew louder as my one-day record against the likes of Pollock and Steyn was very impressive.

But yet again, I was kept out of the team and was on a flight instead to Pune to play the first Ranji match of the season. This was a massive drop. Only two months ago I was leading India!

Anyway I got a hundred in that match and two more hundreds in the season. On the third day of the Ranji match a new team was to be picked. I knew I had to score; otherwise the Kiran Mores of the world would have an easy excuse to drop me.

Things didn't start off well. I lost the toss and Bengal was asked to field. I took five wickets but I still wasn't happy. I knew even five wickets wouldn't merit selection. I made up for it on day three of the game. I had continued to bat from the last session of day two and at lunch remained not out on 175. Mission fulfilled. Now it was up to the selectors.

That very day India were playing South Africa at Eden Gardens. My name flashed on the big screen with the score and apparently the response from the crowd was electrifying. Hearing the cheers, those outside the stadium wondered if Tendulkar had just completed his hundred.

On the basis of my dual performance with the bat and the ball, I was brought back into the team for the first Test match against Sri Lanka in Chennai. I was happy but also realized that from now on I would be on trial the whole time, judged on the basis of each innings. Alone in my hotel room in Pune, I began to wonder how to deal with this intense pressure.

I got home late that night but woke up next morning at seven and went for a run. I thought that was the only way I could prepare for the twenty-two yards. I would train in complete isolation. It would be me and the ball. As I was completing laps one after another I lost count of how long I ran. My mind was focused on the Chepauk track against a deceptive Murali.

Well, Chennai was almost washed out. The teams got a bit of their first innings towards the closing stages of the

Test. I couldn't get my act together and got out cheaply. It only increased the pressure.

At Kotla I got a solid 34 and 37 in the second Test. As I was fighting my battle for survival, the great SRT was surpassing a world record for maximum centuries. What a contrast it must have presented. India won the Test and I thought after being involved in two longish partnerships in the Test I would be retained. Moreover, a winning combination was rarely changed.

Rahul came back from the selection meeting. He took me aside in the dressing room and said, 'Sourav, sorry you are out of the squad.' I was aghast. Again? I was expecting the worst as I felt the plot was thickening around me. But I never expected it would be done in such a manner.

I returned to the hotel and began packing my suitcase. In the meantime, a few teammates heard the news. They immediately came to my room. I could see complete despair on their faces. To be honest, no one else in the period between 2000 and 2006 faced such treatment. Chappell ensured that it had to be Ganguly and only Ganguly.

As I boarded a flight back to Kolkata with my wife and daughter, I felt a small sense of comfort. The crisis had clearly shown me who my true supporters and friends were. I could see that Gambhir, Yuvraj, Bhajji, Sachin, VVS and Sehwag did not approve of the decision. Their respect and love for me were clearly in display. Sachin, for instance, had looked at me with complete bewilderment as he heard the news of my exclusion. 'I have got nothing to say, Dada,' was all that he could murmur.

I was told that I had to return to the Ranji circuit and

prove my credentials yet again. My next match was at Eden Gardens where I narrowly missed getting a hundred. I scored 95 on a green top. India meanwhile went on to win the series. The team for Pakistan was to be announced a few days later. I knew I wasn't going to make it and yet to my utter surprise got selected. Perhaps my recent form and my past record against Pakistan were considered.

Excited, I calculated that the team would be playing only one warm-up game before the first Test in Lahore and that I needed to score in that. I was completely unprepared for the next shock. I received a mail from the board which stated that since all sixteen chosen wouldn't get a chance to play the first warm-up match, five of them would be staying back in India. During this time they would play the Ranji and reach Pakistan just hours before the first Test. I was among those five.

I was surprised. This was never the practice for an overseas tour. Moreover, how could a senior pro like me be kept out in India? I realized I didn't figure in their scheme of things for the first Test. Pakistan had a ferocious pace attack spearheaded by Shoaib. How on earth would I benefit playing Tamil Nadu at Eden Gardens? Their attack would on any given day be 30 kilometres slower than Pakistan's.

At night I found it difficult to sleep. One part of my brain said, it is useless fighting like this. Chappell is out to get you. Pakistan could be the end if you fail even once. The other part of my brain said, don't quit. Quitters never win and you know you have ability on your side.

When I landed in Pakistan it was almost freezing. I remembered my last trip to Inzamamland – it was historic and exceptional. At the end of the tour a special Air India aircraft was commissioned by the Government of India to bring back the victorious team. By the time we checked out of the Marriott Rawalpindi the celebrations had begun even in Pakistan – you would be forgiven for thinking that it was our host country who had won the series.

I happened to be the victorious captain of that team. Then I had felt on top of the world. And today I had no place in the team. I tried motivating myself. I told myself that this country had given me some unforgettable moments to cherish and this time would be no exception. I revisited my past successes while I batted. I was trying to create a successful environment within me by saying I was ready. Cricket, at the end of the day, is a mental sport and I wanted to keep my mind at its best. But it was an uphill struggle and I didn't always succeed.

We were asked to report at the practice ground on the same afternoon of our arrival. I checked into the hotel, quickly changed into my training kit and was at the lobby on time. I have never been so apprehensive, so nervous before a practice session. I met the players and some of them looked happy to see me. I felt that I still belonged to this team. I quickly changed into my whites and was asked to pad up. I knew my Test match was starting at the nets. I batted really well that day.

Practice over, we went back to the hotel by bus. I occupied the second seat on the left which in the Indian team bus was always unofficially mine. Seats on the team bus are usually fixed like the batting order. Sachin used to take the front seat. I used to be right behind him on the left. Even though I was in and out of the team, second seat on the left was reserved for me.

I hadn't completely relaxed despite the good practice session. All the way to the hotel I wondered about the likely batting order. I wasn't sure what the combination would be: Dravid at 3, Sachin 4, Laxman 5, Yuvraj 6? If that was so I didn't quite understand where I fit in.

We arrived at Gaddafi the day before the test. I was taken to a corner by Dravid and Chappell. Surprise of surprises. First they congratulated me on my performance in the Ranji Trophy. Then they asked me whether I would open.

I said I was ready without batting an eyelid. I said I had opened in innumerable one-day games. Had batted at number 3 in Test matches. So I would be perfectly comfortable. To be honest, I was doubtful but I did not let the management feel that. I sent a signal instead that I was ready to adjust to anything to suit the needs of the team.

Some of you may find yourselves in a similar situation. Never ever think that by agreeing to a difficult demand you are belittling yourself. You should look at it, instead, as an opportunity to climb back to the top. Opportunities are not couriered across to you every day. They surface once in a while and when they do you must grab them. Otherwise someone else will gladly accept it and thank you for the free gift. I believed I could succeed. I had no choice. You may not either. Just fasten your seat belts and be ready to fly.

I also knew from my experience as captain that no one comes in the team with a fixed batting order. I thought about the Champions Trophy in Nairobi where I gave the new ball to a left-handed pacer ahead of the more experienced fast bowler. The result was a gentleman called Zaheer Khan. I put Sehwag as an opener in the Lord's Test match and since then he had not put a foot wrong. I realized this unexpected reshuffle in the batting order could also open up unforeseen opportunities for me. So why not give it all that I had? That's how champions were created after all. Sehwag, Hayden, Tendulkar. I decided they might kill me with the new ball but I would not backtrack.

I actually started believing I would be able to counter the storm. So will you. When you climb a hill just visualize you have already reached the top and you will. A lot of people asked me how I hit such big sixes. The answer is simple. I visualized the ground was small and took the long off and long on fielder out of the game. Take the fears out of your life and see how far you reach.

On the day of the match, after the warm-ups, I saw Dravid signalling for me. Greg was standing beside him. I geared up for the worst.

But Dravid explained that he felt it was unfair to push someone like me who had no previous experience of Test match opening. So they had reslotted my batting order to number 5. I stood between them, startled, trying to come to terms with what they had just said.

Dravid was a purist. Especially in Test cricket. He would always approach a game in the most classical way. He and Greg told me that, since I was staging a comeback, sending me up front would send a wrong signal. People might think that I was being sacrificed unfairly.

I wasn't prepared to accept this. Just to accommodate me, the whole batting order had to be rearranged at the last minute. Besides I knew if I succeeded as an opener it would have created fresh opportunities for me to stay afloat rather than fearing whether I'd be selected or not. I argued that the team's interest was paramount and that one player should not be given extra importance. I also said that I was mentally ready to open.

We kept on talking without realizing that the entire incident was being picked up by the electronic media. It went viral. The next day's papers would report our discussion in greater detail than the first day's play. But what I read in the papers was nothing like what had taken place. Let me disappoint the rumour-mongers here – there was no heated argument and only a plain cricketing discussion on the eleven.

I didn't get to bat in the entire Test match as Dravid–Sehwag put up a sensational 400-plus opening stand. This had never happened in my entire career – that I didn't get to bat even a single ball. My only contribution in the Test was a high catch in the outfield.

The second Test match was at Faisalabad, where in an attempt to win the match India went in with five bowlers and I ended up serving drinks. The last time I was dropped in a Test match despite being in the squad was back in 1997, in the Guyana Test. So the experience of accompanying the drinks trolley was almost new to me.

Strangely the exclusion at Faisalabad didn't depress me to the extent I thought it would. The shock after the Zimbabwe series and exclusion at Kotla had hardened me. Dona, who had accompanied me to Pakistan, didn't show any emotion around the removal either. During the Chappell episode she had been confused and upset, but she had clearly toughened. A week later I got picked for the last Test match at Karachi.

Pakistan had prepared a pace-friendly wicket. India started strong with Irfan Pathan getting a hat trick. But the hosts got out of jail and scored around 250 runs.

Then Mohammad Asif with an outstanding spell turned the match on its head. However, for me the spell of the day came from the maverick Shoaib Akhtar. His pace that day was possibly the quickest I have ever handled in international cricket. A bouncer he aimed at my head not only flew past me but went over the keeper's head in one bounce to hit the sight screen.

In my analysis, I batted well in both innings and got 40 and 39. In the second innings I was also involved in a century partnership with Yuvraj, who hit a smashing hundred. For me the big disappointment was that I could not convert two good starts in both innings into a big score. Mentally it was one of the toughest Tests I had ever played. Subsequently, India lost the match and surrendered the series that my team had won here last time.

During the last Test, the team for the one-dayers was announced and as expected the Ganguly surname was missing. I left the port city the day after the last Test match. I was too upset and needed to get away. A voice in my head kept saying, why couldn't I have got a big score and sealed my place? The other said they were out to get you, irrespective of how you played. Did you really think the twin efforts in Karachi and the gritty innings at Kotla were reason enough for a removal? This is one hell of a nasty battle which can't just be fought with a bat.

When I got dropped from the team even the administrative manager of the side in Pakistan, the venerable Raj Singh Dungarpur, seemed surprised. Raj bhai was frank and often outspoken. In the past he had quite often spoken against me. He was like that. Very bindaas. But now he said, how could you leave out Sourav from the one-day team? But even his words cut no ice with the coach, who was clearly running the show.

I reached Kolkata confused. Then I told myself that in the last three months I may have got dropped twice. But it was also true that whenever I got an opportunity I showed that I was still competition-worthy. The rejections had not undone my cricketing abilities. Another thing that heartened me was that the number of my supporters across the country was rapidly increasing.

Look, I was the captain of India for five years. I was one of the stars, a popular face in India. I already had a substantial fan base. But this downhill phase of mine suddenly endeared me to the masses. Even in the media, people who had criticized me routinely turned softer. Suddenly from Maharaj I had joined the ranks of the oppressed.

Sitting at my Behala residence I thought again and again. I finally decided that however powerful they were, the fight would go on. I quietly whispered to myself, Greg, I won't let you win!

A few years later, Rahul and I were chatting in Bengaluru after the Test match against Pakistan. The script had changed by then. Greg Chappell had resigned. Rahul was no longer the captain. He was also struggling for runs. I, on the other hand, was in peak form and had just finished scoring a fighting 239 against Pakistan in Rahul's home town. He complimented me on my batting and almost as an afterthought said, 'I am sorry, Sourav. Just couldn't play you then.'

I wanted to tell him, never mind; the events of that horrible year had made me super tough. I had emerged as a better player. And was really proud of myself. But I didn't say anything. When you are down, it's best not to protest too much. Let your actions make the statement. Whatever I wanted to say I had already said with my cricket bat.

13

Mera Naam Sourav Ganguly.
Bhule toh Nahin?

The battle with Chappell was the darkest chapter of my cricketing life. It was perhaps the worst-kept secret in India that the India coach was dead against bringing back Sourav Ganguly. Through the media he had even offered me a benefit match. My only hope remained the captain who happened to be my deputy for five years and a close friend.

I remember calling Dravid twice on the phone and asking him what the way forward for me was. If I recall correctly the first call was in April and the next was in June 2006. The captain had told me that it was not the end of the road and that my time would come. But nothing changed. Selection meetings would be held every now and then. New replacements would come in. But invariably someone else would be picked ahead of me. I failed to understand what this was about. Ability or something else?

Whatever the problem was, the message was crystal clear. If Chappell remained in the team there was no chance for me. The team eventually got picked by five selectors influenced by the all-powerful coach. For that group I was persona non grata irrespective of what the rest of India thought.

I even had a one-on-one meeting with the then board supremo Sharad Pawar. Mr Pawar was extremely kind to me and I have not forgotten his words. But what he told me was hard to digest. He said, 'Personally I have a good impression about you. But the coach tends to think otherwise. He says you are a disruptive influence on the team.'

I was hurt by the accusation and became slightly emotional. I said, sir, why don't you find out from my colleagues whether there has been any disruption because of me? I have been the captain of this team for five years and now suddenly I have become a disruptive force? I have built this team brick by brick. Have sacrificed my batting slots. Have often fought with opposition captains so that they take Indians seriously. Have led India in almost 200 games. And now suddenly I am being branded as a disruptive force?

Mr Pawar said, 'I believe you. But to be absolutely sure I will have to speak to the team members.' I later wondered whether his conversation with Sachin had led to my inclusion for the Pakistan tour. I never found out. Mr Pawar, however, was a one-time lifeline – now used and gone. I could not keep bothering him. It was not right. But I will always hold close to my heart the fairness with which Mr Pawar handled the situation.

Having exhausted all my options, I wondered whether there was any light at the end of the tunnel. At home the situation was tense. My wife didn't say anything but her demeanour was sombre. I would see astrologers coming in and out of our house to advise my mother. She started believing that wearing a certain ring or a taga (piece of thread) was the only way to change my fortune. I did not.

My father rarely discussed professional matters with me. But one evening he brought up a newspaper report which suggested that after the Indian team's one-day series win in the West Indies, the doors were closed on me forever. I was discussing cricketing matters with Bapi after a long time. It seemed we had gone back to the days when I was a fourteen-year-old, uncertain and eager boy and he my mentor.

He felt that every time India won a cricket match, my chances of getting back to the team appeared slimmer. He said, 'Maharaj, you have achieved a lot. Why don't you walk away with pride?' His voice was full of concern and filled with sadness. It made me feel even more helpless. Finally he came out and said what he was trying hard not to say. 'Maharaj, trust me, I don't see any window for you. Sadly, there is no hope.'

It was a very moving conversation between father and son. My father is no more but I vividly recall what I had told him. I said, no one can play forever. The all-time greats, be it a Maradona, Sampras or Gavaskar, had to stop some day. I do know I will have to go sooner or later. But I do not want to live with the thought that I did not try hard enough, when the chips were down. I made a decision that I shall keep on fighting till I find it impossible to continue. Yes, I do have the easy option of retirement. Of enjoying the fortune that I have made. But I do not want to relax for the rest of my life sitting on a sofa and thinking that I did not give my best. That day I really will go down in my own eyes.

My dad was very supportive of whatever I did in life and he just nodded. Deep down I knew he was not convinced. Conversation over, I returned to my room. I told myself that night, Sourav Ganguly, give yourself one more year and see what happens. I made three decisions that night.

I shall train the hardest.

I will play in all the Ranji matches this season.

I am not going to give up.

By then I had hired a personal trainer. I would train with him six days a week. Fifty per cent of the training was to get myself fit. The other 50 per cent was spent in getting the anger out of my system. I remember one afternoon at Eden Gardens, I ran twenty laps around the ground. Can you believe that the last five or six laps were done almost on autopilot? I was so engrossed in my thoughts that I had become completely unmindful of how much I was running. I am still very thankful to my trainer, Goutam Roy, who was available any time of the day or night, whenever I needed him. Due to such strenuous training I lost about 9 kilos without even touching the bat.

It was an amazing situation to be in. My mind was split into three. One, tremendous belief in my own ability. Two, unsure about my comeback possibilities. Three, as my father had said, growing pessimism with every Indian win.

I did see statements made in the press by one or two of my dear colleagues supporting my claim in the eleven. It certainly did not please the all-powerful coach and both were warned by the BCCI and one of them was served a show-cause notice. I felt touched but did not know whether it was proper to text them. Or to call up and say thank you. I found the setting completely unreal.

The Champions Trophy came along. This time India was hosting it. Now this is a tournament where my performance was possibly the best among the current group of Indian players. Yet, as expected, I did not get selected. It hurt all the more as the tournament was played on my home soil. My cricketing outings remained limited to leading Bengal in the Ranji Trophy. It was not easy playing in front of half-empty galleries, staying in hotels which offered little comfort, playing against opposition teams which were light years away from the international standard.

Around this time I got a call from the Pepsi boss in India to appear in a commercial which would be based around my current predicament. He said they hadn't seen a bigger public outcry over the exclusion of one player. Brand Pepsi wanted to support my cause and take it to the people.

I refused. I didn't want to be party to such melodrama. Nor did I want any sympathy by participating in a campaign where I had to say stuff like, 'Mein Sourav Ganguly hoon. Bhule toh nahin? Jo hua kyon hua? Kaise hua?' ending with a heartfelt 'Hawa mein shirt ghoomane ke liye aur ek mauka mil jaye?'

Pepsi wasn't pleased with my refusal. One day I got a legal notice saying that Pepsi had the right to decide on the script as long as it didn't tarnish my image as a brand. So I had to do the ad. But I was hesitant and found it extremely awkward to say those emotional lines.

I wasn't prepared for the sensational viewers' response

that followed. When it was aired on TV, I was flooded with letters and messages. Ganguly versus Chappell became a national debate.

What turned public opinion increasingly in my favour was the fact that India lost in South Africa. They ended up losing the one-day series 1-4. The performance led to discussions in Parliament. Even the coach got involved in a heated exchange with members of Parliament sitting thousands of miles away.

The Test team for South Africa was to get picked now and my name started featuring on some lists. On the day of the selection I happened to be at Eden Gardens practising. We had just beaten Punjab in an away match. Yet instead of celebrating the win, I was unsure. I told myself, if I was ignored again, it really might be the end. I would lose the urge to fight.

There was no match that day, yet the Eden Gardens lawn remained crowded with media. Sometime in the afternoon, a few journalists shouted, Sourav, you have been picked. Half in disbelief, half ecstatic, I just raised my hands.

It was an unbelievable feeling. I was like a child who had been gifted his first chocolate box. It was a deep and complete feeling of joy. I felt like I was earning my first India cap. The city too shared my euphoria.

Meanwhile, I received a call from a journalist covering the South Africa series. He didn't seem very happy with my selection. Like a well-meaning uncle, he could only mutter, 'Very happy that you got picked. But why did you work tirelessly towards getting selected in this series? This is a huge mistake. The South Africans are in devastating form. You should have timed your comeback intelligently to coincide with the West Indies series at home. That would have been much safer for you.'

I disagreed. I was determined to go to South Africa. My logic was simple. If I wanted to restore my place in the Indian team for another three or four years I had to perform in the toughest of conditions. I felt that South Africa in that era presented the toughest of conditions, tougher than England and Australia. In Mandelaland the wickets were also much quicker. The ball used to seam a lot. Wickets like Durban offered solid bounce. And in such conditions, the South African team's bowling attack was the best in the world.

It was a now-or-never kind of a situation and I couldn't afford to slip up. Thus began some excruciating days of practice. I would finish my nets with the Bengal team at the Jadavpur University ground in Salt Lake and then head towards Eden Gardens to get into the Indoor Practice Hall. There I would practise with hard plastic balls to get used to the bounce and the additional pace. I also did a fair bit of parachute training to get fitter.

I had to get to Potchefstroom, where a warm-up match was scheduled before the first Test. On board I noticed a few TV crew members. They didn't cover the one-dayers but were now obviously going long distance to cover the likely TRP-raising spectacle. This would not be about India versus South Africa but Ganguly versus Chappell. I did not want this.

The local manager was at Joburg airport to receive me and the three other new members of the Test team. He said the management wanted me to attend the practice straight away. I realized the match had already begun. But I also remembered what I had told my father. I still had cricket left in me!

14

Out of Jail at Wanderers

I had once asked Gavaskar, how did you manage to play those marathon innings for six–seven hours when the practice session at the nets never exceeded forty minutes? The answer was mind-blowing.

Gavaskar said it was not the batting duration at the nets that was responsible for your staying power at the crease. It was the visualization process that prepared a batsman for the real thing. You had to be in the zone that convinced the mind that you were battling session after session and in the process getting a big hundred.

A batsman also has to find a way to relax and be ready when he stands at the batting end. The mind has amazing power. Which provides you the energy and stamina to carry on. Preparation is also essential. Mind you, preparation never begins at the nets or in the dressing room.

It begins in the bus, in the hotel room, at your friend's party or during a walk down the beach. They say you improve the most when you don't have to appear for exams the next day. You become better while resting as your mind is at its best when it is at peace. It's so true.

I tried following the same tactics in South Africa.

Whatever I did, my mind was constantly focused on a single mission. To deliver a big Test match performance. I got hit so many times in my dreams. Got beaten by a beauty but in no time I would gather myself and clobber that short delivery to the point boundary.

I had countless batting exercises stored in my mind from my experience of playing more than a hundred Test matches. It was like carrying a video recorder in my head. All I had to do was push the play button.

I remembered what Desmond Haynes had taught me several years ago at the beginning of my career in England. Keep thinking positive. Keep visualizing your success. If you think you will nick outside the off stump, chances are that you will. He said, the best innings of your life will be the ones when you go to bed thinking of success and believing in success. Haynes was a brilliant batsman who had successfully combatted the best fast bowlers in the world but even he would fail whenever he allowed himself to feel even an iota of fear.

It was very important to succeed in the warm-up match and make a statement right from the word go. I knew I was on trial. It will happen to you as well if you are in a competitive world. Nobody escapes the ups and downs of life. At some stage you will face such a challenge. My advice is to look at such a challenge as an opportunity. Embrace it.

The truth is that the best in the world look at the toughest of situations as an opportunity to become famous. Do remember champions are never born or created under normal circumstances. Calamities create winners. The best take up challenges which seem impossible. The weak never do. That ultimately makes the difference.

My opening examination started a few hours after I landed from a long flight, in a relatively unknown place called Potchefstroom, which is a little more than 100 kilometres from Johannesburg. A car took us there directly from Joburg airport. Once we reached, I went directly to the practice arena.

I tried to remain calm and set aside my apprehensions. There was no point in panicking. Rather, it was important to create my own mental space to succeed. At the nets the coach came and shook hands with me. I knew that his politeness was only skin-deep. For him to have faith in my abilities was like expecting mutton biryani in Somalia.

I was asked to pad up quickly. As I was putting on the straps I had a very strange feeling. I knew the exam was beginning in the next few minutes. And that I either performed or perished.

By the time I finished wearing my pads captain Dravid appeared on the scene. We shook hands. He said, 'It is good to have you back. Hopefully you will have some good scores.' I could understand where he was coming from. After having lost the one-day series so badly as captain, he was in desperate need of a bit of sunshine.

As we made small talk about the domestic season, I felt that my old colleague and friend was trying to gauge my state of mind. Perhaps I am imagining things. But I felt he was conveying a message to me – you have played here so many times, and know the conditions so well, he seemed to be saying. I look forward to you making a difference.

I looked at his face closely and said to myself, welcome to the world of captains. It only gets tougher with time. Then I almost pinched myself. Sourav Ganguly, don't think about such things. You better focus. You have to understand life has changed.

While Rahul was talking to me, my mind travelled elsewhere. I was thinking about negotiating bowlers properly at the nets and making a mark. It was almost unreal that even after playing international cricket non-stop for ten years, one particular day's net practice could assume so much importance. But that's the way it was.

As I was about to enter the nets I saw fast bowlers had been handed the new ball. I looked around and saw batsmen at the other nets using chest pads. I had the chest pad in my kitbag but was hesitant to use it. Everyone was watching me closely and I decided not to use so much protective equipment. I wanted to send a silent message that I was fearless and completely battle ready.

I had decided at the beginning of the tour that I might get hit. I might break a bone. I might get killed. But I was not going to take a backward step. I was going to give everything that I had. I batted at the nets and never looked back. I got bounced but kept going forward.

I batted for more than half an hour at the nets. I surprised myself at the way I hit the ball. Your body and mind will react exactly how you train them and I was in excellent shape. It was an amazing lesson. While I was taking off the pads and preparing myself to bowl, the coach came over and said, 'Well batted.' It was almost surreal. As if a teenager had got the special nod of approval from his school headmaster. The net session was not recorded in cricket history books, but to my mind, it was as good a performance as any I have had.

Practice over, we returned to the hotel. At the hotel lobby I asked Sachin and Zaheer what they were doing for lunch. They said they were going to a nearby restaurant called Spurs. I joined them there. I was trying to get back into the team mode. Signalling that I was like just another cricketer and carried no baggage.

It is never easy for a captain who has led these players for more than five years to behave like a budding player. But the circumstances were such that I had to do a complete role reversal. I was also training myself to get used to this. The past was the past. Professional life is all about remaining in the present.

We ordered chicken and steaks. During lunch I asked how the team was shaping up. How did they lose so badly in the one-day series? I got the impression that all was not well in the team. They didn't look like a very happy family. There were telltale signs of internal strain which I had picked up as soon as I had arrived.

Two days later at the warm-up tie, India lost the toss and was put in to bat. There was barely any grass on the wicket. In no time we were 37 for 3 and I had to go in. Earlier, as I sat in the dressing room waiting for my turn, I had said to myself over and over again, like a mantra:

Sourav, you may get hit.

You may break a bone.

You may die but don't take a backward step.

You are not playing for your wicket.

You are playing for your pride.

No point in living life if you lose your pride.

The opposition had four fast bowlers and all of them were trying to create a spot for themselves in the Test eleven. It took me a few overs to get adjusted to the pace and bounce of the South African wickets. It was a bowler-friendly track and I knew if we managed to put up a decent total we could win.

Well, India won the match in three days. What made me extra happy was that I got a fighting 83 and remained a major contributor to the victory. When I got out and was returning to the dressing room I saw everyone standing at the balcony and clapping. A teammate even said, this is the Ganguly of old.

The team meanwhile had started a new practice of a cardio session after the day's play. If you got runs and spent enough time at the crease, you were exempted from that. The trainer had excused me but I was in no mood to indulge in such liberties and completed the twenty-minute session effortlessly. I wanted to show how much I had improved.

We reached Johannesburg to play the first Test. I knew despite my performance in the warm-up match, this presented the real challenge. It was a travelling day, which meant the visiting team got a day off. But despite the holiday I hit the gym. My performance in Potchefstroom would mean nothing if I failed here.

We had practice the next day. I again played my heart out and learnt that I would be in the eleven. We were going in with only Kumble in the spin department as the wicket was a green top. We had the team meeting in the

evening, where I was asked to speak. Several others spoke
before me, and I could tell that this team was lacking in
self-belief. Even the champion Sachin was in an uncertain
and tentative state of mind.

As I spoke, the old Ganguly, the team captain, emerged.
I spoke for about fifteen minutes and urged my colleagues,
saying, come on, we can beat South Africa. I reminded
them of some epic overseas matches where we had fought
under remarkable pressure and won.

This team were doing their net sessions with utmost
sincerity. They did the required laps on the ground. They
were well disciplined. But to win Test matches overseas you
needed something more than that. You needed someone to
tell you that if you had done it once, there was no reason
why you couldn't do it again.

After the meeting, I went directly to Sach's room. He
was someone I could trust completely. Like me he was
also trying to get the team back on track. I had a great
conversation with him. We ordered dinner in his room
and both felt refreshed and ready for the all-important Test
match beginning the next day.

As we drove into the Wanderers I must admit I was very
nervous. Once we arrived at the ground I was very keen on
finding out the team South Africa was picking. It was not
a surprise to know that they had packed five fast bowlers –
Shaun Pollock, Dale Steyn, André Nel, Jacques Kallis and
Makhaya Ntini.

Rahul surprised me big time by electing to bat on a
surface where at times the outfield could not be separated
from the wicket. It had rained quite a bit and the game

started after lunch. When my turn came to bat towards the closing stages of the day's play I had to negotiate a very hostile hour of pace bowling. Captain Graeme Smith was trying to make a statement and rightly so. I remained not out on 14 and at the end of the day's play immediately went into the adjacent indoor nets.

I took assistant coach Ian Frazer along as I wanted him to put the right kind of balls in the bowling machine and adjust it. I particularly wanted to practise against the kind of deliveries a Makhaya Ntini was bowling – back of a length and almost 85 miles an hour. I kept on practising for half an hour and only then boarded the coach.

As we drove back into the Sandton Sun hotel, I rehearsed every ball that had been bowled to me that day. At night I sat alone in my room, watching TV. But my mind was still playing those back of a length deliveries. A kind of mantra was playing in my head:

No one will help you

There won't be any comfort zones

There will be no rest

You will have to be your own hero.

Three years ago, in these very grounds, I had lost the one thing I wanted the most, the World Cup. Today I must avenge that defeat.

I wanted to get a hundred but eventually remained not out on 51 as the innings folded for 249. As I was walking up the stairs in Wanderers, I saw my teammates applauding me. That included the all-powerful coach. I looked at the faces of my teammates. In their eyes I could read a silent message – your batting was brilliant and you were unfairly kept out for the last four months.

Sreesanth then bowled brilliantly to put South Africa under pressure and we ended up winning a Test match in Mandelaland for the first time. The margin was 123 runs. Not bad for a team that had lost the one-day series 1-4 just weeks ago.

Everyone was euphoric. It was as if we had won a major trophy or the series. In the midst of the celebrations, the coach came and congratulated me. I felt he was also under enormous pressure – perhaps he felt that following the row in Parliament, his job was also on the line. This despite enjoying a lucrative contract which extended up to the World Cup.

I knew I had succeeded and made others happy. But deep inside I also knew I still had miles to go. I had not forgotten the incidents of Kotla. By then I had already come to terms with the fact that I wouldn't lead India again. I also realized that I did not miss it. My next priority was to keep on playing for the team and piling up runs.

In competitive sports or in any high-profile job your performance for ten years is only a bonus. It is never a fixed deposit. Once you are done at the top, you may have to climb the ladder from the bottom again. You can't think, I was the leader, I was the decision-maker, I am entitled to get certain advantages. Take it from me that you won't get any advantages and the sooner you get rid of such thoughts the better. The lesson I learnt in those gruelling four months was that the past counted for nothing.

We flew down to Durban. There was a warm-up game before the second Test. My only relief was that I had a bit of rest before the next examination began at the bouncy Kingsmead. At Durban we were staying at the Elengeni, where we had stayed at the World Cup semi-final in 2003. It is beautifully located by the Indian Ocean.

As I walked down the beach by the hotel I realized that the bitterness of the last four months was slowly easing. I was beginning to enjoy playing again without bearing the weight of captaincy. Yes, I was at the mercy of a selection committee for every game. But this had happened to me before, in those early years from 1996 to 2000.

I told myself I was not alone. There were nine other players in the team apart from the captain who would undergo the same process of selection. They too were not guaranteed their places in the side. So why should I fear? It was a remarkable period in my life where with every passing day I felt stronger and braver.

In the Durban Test we failed to put up a fight. My scores in the innings were 0 and 26. Good sides never give up and keep coming at you and that was what the South Africans did. They levelled the series 1-1. The decider was to be played at Cape Town.

The Newlands Cricket Ground has to rank among the prettiest in the world. I had some happy memories of the ground, including getting a hundred in the World Cup. But that was in the past. I knew I had to score here following my failure in Durban.

As we finished a gruelling practice session, the coach

asked us to assemble in the changing room. He had some tough words for the boys, and rightly so. He cautioned the team that it was reckless on our part to lose the plot so completely after winning the first Test. He urged us to be courageous. As I was listening to the team talk I looked at Rahul and Greg. I saw them going through the same pain and anxiety that I had borne all these years.

I requested the captain and coach to allow me to stay back for some additional practice. As the team bus left I went into the nets with Ian Frazer. The nets at Newlands is at the other side, a fair walk, from the dressing room. The reason I went back was that I wanted it to be just me and the bowler. I batted for a good forty minutes. Luckily, none of the local net bowlers had left by then.

As we were about to board the car, Frazer asked, 'Why did you come back again?' I didn't know whether he would understand my reasoning. I also became worried that it would be held against me. Back at the hotel, I couldn't sleep well that night. I got up at one in the morning and stayed awake for the rest of the night.

India won the toss and batted. Wasim Jaffer got a lovely hundred and I didn't get to bat on the first day. The second day when I came out to bat, an express Steyn delivery hit me on the head. I still remember the noise – it was so loud that the big Saturday crowd at Newlands must have heard it. It was a real challenge to continue after that.

The next delivery was the biggest test. I knew if I flinched it would send a signal to the bowler that I had got edgy. Steyn turned to bowl the next delivery which was a full length one. I was right there on the front foot and posted it through the cover to get a two. It was only a two but the effect it had on me was enormous.

I got a fighting 66 and played the second new ball with confidence. In the second innings I scored 46 in a difficult situation when India was struggling at 6 for 2. The chairman of selectors, Dilip Vengsarkar, happened to be there. He was full of praise for me.

The Test was over in four days with India losing the series. We folded up for only 169 in the second innings despite scoring 400-plus in the first. But I quietly told myself that maybe I had earned my one-day place back. I felt I was now a completely different player, someone who could have an international career which would span a few more years.

In the second innings of the Cape Town Test, I was as usual slated to go at number 6. But there was some confusion when the second wicket fell. Tendulkar was going in but the umpire stopped him as he had been out of the field for more than ten minutes.

The current rules of cricket stipulate that if you are out for some amount of time while your team is fielding, the same time span needs to be covered by your team before you are eligible to bat in the next innings.

The Indian innings had not even crossed ten minutes. So Sachin was considered ineligible to bat. The scoreboard was showing 6-2 and I was sitting in the dressing room in whites. The coach came almost running and urged, 'Sourav, quickly pad up and go.'

Mind you, the ball was still new. India was under tremendous pressure.

We were eventually all out for less than 200. That left South Africa a target which was not very difficult to chase. We lost the Test and thereby the series. But I did preserve my new-found belief with a fighting 46 which was the second highest score of the innings after Rahul's 47. What I found particularly pleasing was that the all-powerful coach didn't ask Laxman to handle this pressure situation. Instead he turned to his old enemy. Perhaps I had finally won our battle.

15

High Tide – and the Ebb

Once I asked Shane Warne what the difference was between the South African and Australian teams of his era.

Warne explained it beautifully. 'South Africa was as good as us,' he said in his typical Australian swagger. 'But they approached their cricket differently. While we encouraged the players to express their natural flair, South Africa went into a match with preconceived notions. They were rarely flexible. That's why we hammered them.'

I saw Warne's point. This was exactly what had led to the downfall of Greg Chappell's India. Greg always wanted a certain style of cricket from his team. I remember the series opener in Nagpur when I was staging a comeback in the one-day team. He instructed us to approach the initial overs aggressively, the middle overs normally and then accelerate towards the end. I found it inexplicable.

Our team had finishers of the calibre of Yuvraj, Dhoni and Dravid. Why should they be asked to play in a certain manner? An innings should always progress according to the merit of the attack and on adjustment to the surface. The job of the openers was not only to bat, but to send a message to the dressing room about what was achievable.

The rest of the batting line-up would then adapt themselves to what was unfolding in the field. Fixed ideas constrained the players and I felt we were treading on the wrong path.

If you are introducing a youngster to top-level cricket you need to give him space. I believed in taking the fear of failure away from players. Once you pick someone you need to make him feel that he is the best. He should not worry about what the selectors or coach or media thinks about him. He should think about the ball only. That is how you get the best out of him. It is important to be in the right mindset before a big game. Too much pressure kills you and makes you half the player you are in your natural flow. And the biggest mistake you could make was to sit on a youngster's head. But then I was in no position to effect a change. I was not the leader and had to follow what was told. That too on a Nagpur track which has always been a belter.

It didn't help that Greg also had preconceived notions about people and my name was on the top of the list. From the time I got out of jail at Wanderers till Greg's exit after the World Cup, I had to constantly fight two battles. One, keep scoring runs. Two, handle the prejudices of the coach. To be honest, I wasn't even aware of his prejudices till I read his book.

Anyway, Nagpur was my acid test after having passed the Test match exams in South Africa. You always feel extra confident when you reach your favourite venue. It's purely a psychological thing. At the highest level the game is so much about the mind, and your attitude and feelings make a real difference. But this time the pressure and tension got the better of me.

The night before the match I could not sleep at all. I have never ever advocated the use of sleeping pills. I worried that the hangover would be too much to handle the following morning and affect my game. A meagre five hours' sleep can still keep you fresh. But being groggy with a sleeping pill was a clear-cut recipe for disaster. So I just kept tossing and turning on my bed that night.

Since the management wanted me to play in a certain way I decided to play safe, knowing it was the only way I could survive and stay in the team. As I struggled with my doubts and fears, I wondered if others were going through the same feelings. In Nagpur it was me. After a few months it was the turn of the great Tendulkar, who clearly was not happy being asked to bat at 4 in the World Cup.

But he had to perform this role for the team. During this period I got a welcome breather. Sachin for once became the one who had to face the tyrannies of the coach. It was reassuring to know that my loving mate of so many years and a champion was in the same boat as me.

Back to Nagpur. Dravid won the toss and I was immediately on the field. I should have got a comeback hundred but was run out for 98. We did win the match against a formidable West Indies side which had Gayle, Lara and Chanderpaul in their ranks. I walked away with the Man of the Match award. Not too bad for someone making a comeback after nearly a year in this form of cricket. I also calculated that I had won the most Man of the Match awards in my ten years in the team.

I was also in very good form in the Sri Lanka series that followed. I was congratulated by all the team members including the coach. But by then I had trained my mind in such a way that even the applause didn't matter. I knew my bat was the only reliable friend that existed on this earth. The runs and the awards of course ensured that I was no longer treated as an outlaw.

Under Greg the atmosphere was so gloomy that even after playing an important role in two back-to-back series victories I was still not a hundred per cent sure of my place in the World Cup team. Most of the team members were equally apprehensive. Finally, the squad was announced and I did get a place. But even when we were mid-air, my apprehensions hadn't subsided. I desperately wanted to excel in this tournament as I still had points to prove and I wanted the team to do well.

Deep down I wondered if we were mentally strong enough to take off. My fears sadly turned out to be true as we had the most disastrous World Cup. The team had in their ranks some of the best players in one-day cricket. But it was also a team plagued by too much self-doubt. We were so lacklustre that we ended up losing against Bangladesh in the opening tie. We recovered slightly against Bermuda. Then washed away our final hope by crashing out against Sri Lanka and failing to qualify for the second round. It was a classy team but a scared outfit.

I got two half-centuries in the three innings that I played. In the overall scenario, my 66 and 89 in the first two matches weren't unimpressive at all. However, it meant very little as the team couldn't fulfil the expectations even one bit. I was devastated. So was the rest of the team. This was easily the darkest moment of my playing career.

The outcry in India was huge. The nation failed to come to terms with our terrible performance. I still remember a middle-aged Indian fan. He was so shattered that he pushed the media aside and came running to us in the grounds. It was very upsetting to see what our defeat had done to fans like him.

Even Sachin's home was not spared. According to news reports, people held demonstrations outside his place and shouted slogans against him. This had never happened during his glittering international career. For a man who had brought so much fame to the country it was immensely disturbing. And uncalled for. The houses of some other team members were also targeted.

From Port of Spain, the team took the same flight to London. But from there, we departed to our individual destinations. I stayed back in London with the family. The idea was to get away from the madness. And things were mad. In India I discovered that my Bangladesh innings of 66 in 129 balls was put down to a special bat contract I had with Puma which paid me by how much time I spent in the crease. This was why I had apparently scored less than a run a ball.

The report ignored the glaring fact that in the Bangladesh match, at one stage, we were tottering at 40-3, having lost Sehwag, Sachin and Uthappa in quick succession. When Rahul got out, the score was 72-4 and we worried whether the innings would fold up in 40 overs. How on earth could I have accelerated in such conditions? But then fertile minds will always create fertile stuff.

Under normal circumstances I may have ignored the

loose talk, but we were sitting on a minefield. Emotions in the country were really charged. I had to react and clarify. So I wrote to the board to deny the report, attaching a copy of my Puma contract. Indian cricket was in a complete mess. Suspicion, insecurity and gloom prevailed everywhere.

The clouds cleared the moment Greg Chappell was asked to go. Our new coaches were Ravi Shastri in Bangladesh and then Chandu Borde in England. Overnight it was a different dressing room with the same bunch of boys. I even found a different Dravid. He was relaxed, friendlier, and seemed for the first time enjoying his tenure as captain.

For a welcome change no video camera was recording our activities in the dressing room. Believe me, our Australian coach would bring a cameraperson to record the team activities on video. I found it outrageous. I have no idea why he did that. Was it to create some documentation for him? Whatever the reason, the players didn't take it too kindly. They found it a massive invasion of privacy.

As I look back on the Chappell era in Indian cricket, I still find it difficult to comprehend. It felt like such a waste. Greg had the opportunity to serve Indian cricket for a long time and leave a legacy but he did exactly the opposite, destroying a team and cutting short his tenure. A coach has to be a team's friend. With his man management skills he should find a way to extract the best from the players. But Greg had no clue about man management and that was why he messed up big time. He ended up being the unsuccessful boss whom almost everyone hated.

After the World Cup we toured Bangladesh and won the Test series easily. Sachin and I were rested in the one-day series. But we were back in the Tests and both got a hundred in Chittagong. During our long partnership we kept on joking that we must perform or bite the bullet.

Next on the schedule was the England tour where we ended up winning a series after twenty-one years. I performed very well with both the bat and the ball. Before reaching England we played South Africa in Ireland and won. A team that failed to beat Bangladesh accounted for South Africa in Ireland. What stood out for me was the complete performance reversal pre- and post-Chappell.

I must make a special mention of our manager on the English tour, Chandu Borde. At the outset his selection had surprised many. Yes, he was not getting any younger and couldn't be very energetic. Yet his strategic inputs on the tour were enormous. The best thing Borde did was to keep the players in a good frame of mind.

Every team meeting on that tour ended with a round of laughter and claps. He made some amazingly positive statements about the players on tour. He was full of praise for my bowling, which encouraged me a lot. He knew I was in the team as a batsman but by appreciating my bowling he gave me so much confidence that it reflected in my batting.

The day Dravid lifted the series winner's Pataudi Trophy at the Oval, my joy knew no bounds. India had won a series against England after twenty-one years and I felt so proud to be part of that history. So when he decided to suddenly retire after these triumphs it came as a complete surprise. I thought the team was bonding well under him. They were in a relaxed state of mind and the dressing room was back to how it had been. Why did he decide to go?

Rahul has never really spoken about it. My understanding is that he may have felt that the pressures of captaincy reflected in his batting. Batting with Rahul at the Oval during the penultimate day's play of the Test series, I had noticed he was a shadow of his former self.

We could have enforced a follow-on and put England under additional pressure as they were already trailing 0-1 in the series. Dravid's decision not to do this was reasonable, but I failed to understand what lay behind his ultra-slow batting in the second innings on a friendly Oval surface.

India were 11-3 when I joined him at the wicket. I got out when the score was 76-4. I had made a quickfire 50-plus and at the other end Rahul was painstakingly slow. I have the highest admiration for Rahul and also understand that there are days when nothing goes right for you.

On that particular day he struggled to hit a ball of the square. At one point I wondered if it was really Rahul at the other end. When I got out for 57 off 68 balls, he had barely made 10. Eventually he got 12 off 96 balls. At one stage he had scored 2 off 52 balls. This was unthinkable for a batsman who has won so many matches for India.

Having led the side for more than five years, I perfectly understood his problems. The burden of captaincy gets harder to bear over time. Contrary to conventional thinking, it is much easier when you are starting the job. The biggest challenge for a leader is to stay in the present. I saw a different Dravid that day as he was thinking well ahead of the game. His mind was preoccupied with the result. The same Dravid without the burden of captaincy was brilliant in 2011 and went on to score four centuries in his last series in England.

After England we played Pakistan at home. I was immensely successful in the series, scoring my maiden hundred at Eden Gardens. I followed it up at Chinnaswamy with a double century in my 99th Test match. I was not only the Player of the Match but walked away with the Player of the Series trophy as well.

Today when I think of how my fortunes swung from 2006 to 2007, I come to the conclusion that it was more than a roller-coaster ride. A coach had demoted my status to a water boy in Faisalabad and the same team then utilized my services the very next year as the series winner. Against the same team. Even when things are not working for you, don't quit. Just hang in there. Darkness also has an expiry date.

But for me, there is always a twist in the tale. Whenever the sun shines on me, it's never long before clouds gather again. At times I have been quietly confident and the next morning discovered how misplaced that confidence was.

We were touring Australia under Anil Kumble and the first Test match of the series presented a huge landmark for me. It was my 100th Test match. The youngster who had started off his Test match career at Lord's did not know then that one day he would record this feat at the oldest cricket ground in the world. It was a dream come true.

We lost the match by a huge margin by batting badly. Our batting line-up could only score 196 and 161. I did put up a fight with 43 and 40 in the two innings but that was not good enough. We went into the Sydney Test with high hopes as SCG was traditionally good to us. It was on this historic ground that Steve Waugh, in his final battle, had prevented us from beating Australia and clinched the series.

The Indian team under Kumble had also pinned their hopes on Sydney to turn things around. We started off pretty well in the Test match and few could have predicted the end would be so dismal under highly controversial circumstances. That test match has become infamous as the 'Monkeygate' test.

During the test, Andrew Symonds had claimed that he was racially abused by Harbhajan and called a monkey. Not many will know that things were hotting up from the very first day of the Test. We were convinced that Symonds was caught behind with the scorecard showing 134-6. Had he been given out we may have won the Test. But they went on to score 461. Symonds got a big hundred. The face of the match changed completely.

Things got ugly with the cricket boards getting involved. The Indian team even wanted to pull out of the series. We felt the match referee was unfair and Bhajji was getting subjected to all sorts of threats. At that crucial stage, captain Kumble along with a very vocal Laxman and a couple of us stood up. Finally the crisis was avoided. And we went on to win the next Test at Perth.

I did my bit in Sydney as well, scoring 67 and 51. In the second innings my catch was controversially claimed by Michael Clarke. Michael today happens to be a good friend of mine.

If losing the Test match was a team disaster, a bigger one awaited me. I was so confident of my place in the tri-nation one-day series that was to follow that I had brought along the extra light blue one-day pads in my kitbag. There was absolutely no doubt in my mind that I would get picked.

The night before the selection, a Kolkata journalist called on my Australia number. He told me that my one-day place was not a certainty. I found this outrageous. I said, I have not only scored in all four Test innings of the series but performed most consistently for the Indian team this season. Look, last year I was the third highest one-day run-getter in the world after Kallis and Sangakkara. You are saying they will drop me? Impossible!

But he was right. Next afternoon, when the team was announced, Rahul and I were dropped. I never played for the Indian one-day team again.

16

Life with Shah Rukh

The Indian Premier League-4 auction was coming up. And as they say, there was a nip in the air. The media were speculating about my future with the Kolkata Knight Riders (KKR). Meanwhile, I had a visitor in my old office at Park Street.

Venky Mysore, KKR's newly appointed CEO, had sent a KKR representative to meet me. He came to the point rather quickly. He seemed a little embarrassed as he said, 'Sourav, this season we can't keep you as a player. But we would be very happy if you take up the job of mentoring KKR.'

I said I needed to think about the offer. I knew my answer, but still took some time to give my official response. I could have called up the owner directly. But I resisted. I had known Shah Rukh Khan for a long time and enjoyed a friendship with him. But it was not rocket science that the offer must have had his approval.

If memory serves me right, the first time I met Shah Rukh was in Mumbai around 2000. Nimbus, the then official broadcasters of the BCCI, had organized a glamour-packed award function night. Shah Rukh was hosting it. I was called on stage to give away an award.

Of course I knew him through his movies. But this was the first time I experienced his boundless energy, ready wit and magnetism. Shah Rukh also seemed very cordial. I was very impressed. Subsequently we would meet on and off. I would say we had also developed a kind of friendship.

When I was leading India in the South Africa World Cup, amid the team's roller-coaster ride we were in constant touch. Shah Rukh himself was going through a tough time. He was recuperating from a back surgery in London. He would regularly encourage the team through his texts to me and I would reciprocate. Being a sportsman myself, I knew how injuries and operations can dent the confidence of top-quality professionals. When he got better, he thanked me for being with him during the troubled times in a touching SMS.

In 2008, while we were touring Australia for a keenly contested series, I received a call from Lalit Modi one night. We were in Adelaide. What Lalit told me was quite encouraging.

He said Shah Rukh has bought the Kolkata franchise and I as the former Indian captain must guide him all the way. I said, that goes without saying. Lalit also informed me that I would be leading the Kolkata franchise.

I was eagerly looking forward to the challenge. I was one of the few Indian players who had experience of playing T20 cricket as it was by then a very popular format in England and my tenure at Northampton and Glamorgan had already introduced me to it. I would love to have participated in the inaugural T20 World Cup. But captain Dravid convinced us to withdraw from the tournament. He said he had opted out. I followed him. So did Sachin.

The year was 2007. We had just beaten England in England. It was, as I said earlier, a truly historic win and Dravid understandably seemed very happy. In 1996, on our maiden tour to England both Rahul and I had felt that the team was playing second fiddle to the hosts. A decade on, Dravid's team had effected a sea change.

He spoke to us at the end of the series. He said we had achieved something that had remained unattainable and that we must think of future challenges. He suggested that we take a break from the T20 World Cup and concentrate on the very important next season, which would involve a daunting Pakistan.

Little did I know that Dravid himself would be stepping down from captaincy within a few days. During the discussion he did not even drop a hint that he would be quitting. If he had done that I would not have opted out of the T20 World Cup. After getting dropped from the one-day team during the Chappell era, I had decided that I would not take rest and play whatever I was offered. All performers, remember one thing: there is no tomorrow in the professional world. Every day is about that day – It's not about the future or the past. If you choose a particular path in life there should be no breaks till you decide to give up. Give your all or else someone else will.

Back to the first IPL. I went to Shah Rukh's house the night before the auction. I found John Buchanan there, and Andrew Leipus and Adrian Le Roux, the well-known

South African physio-trainer pair. Buchanan had already been appointed coach of the team by the KKR management.

I had not heard hugely complimentary things about John Buchanan from some of the Australian players. Warne's opinion about him was public knowledge. I had gone with my wish list of 17–18 players. John had his own list. The format for picking players at the auction was completely different from what I had encountered in the past. We went into the auction and picked players.

The good part was that the KKR family seemed very cordial. Apart from Shah Rukh there was Jai Mehta, the co-owner, and his wife, the ever-smiling Juhi Chawla. I have always had a lot of respect for Shah Rukh, who is a self-made achiever. I had heard about how he went to Mumbai from Delhi with absolutely zero reference, and fought and won a battle on his own and became one of the greatest superstars.

I found his life hugely inspirational. Especially the story of his buying 'Mannat', the sprawling mansion overlooking the Arabian Sea where he resides. Apparently as a struggling actor he used to sit on the benches around the seafront overlooking the house. He told himself, one day this will be mine. I found it remarkable that our team owner could chase his dreams so successfully.

The players were really inspired by his presence. However, Shoaib Akhtar took it to another level. He seemed mesmerized in SRK's company. I asked him one day, why do you keep staring at him? His answer had me in splits. Shoaib said, 'I keep on thinking, is he the same man who holds the hands of some of the most gorgeous women in Bollywood? Jumps from a running train? Fights with twenty people and roams around in the rose gardens?'

A few days with Shoaib showed me that this man had something more than cricket in him. He viewed the world through his own lens and often came up with some extremely amusing observations. Sometimes I find myself laughing out aloud when I replay some of the Shoaib specials.

I will always remember our first meeting in Adelaide. Shoaib would have only played eight to ten international matches then. In the previous match the Pakistan captain was fined heavily for slow over rate. Much of it was happening because the fast bowlers especially Shoaib took so much time to send down an over.

I asked him if he would shorten his run-up in the next match. Shoaib was surprised. He said, 'Come on. They [Waqar and Wasim] can think of reducing it. I can't. A Boeing 777 needs a runway to fly.'

Our first match was in Bengaluru against Royal Challengers Bangalore (RCB). It was the opening match of the IPL. Judging by the atmosphere the entire city seemed caught up in the IPL frenzy. I was stunned when I went out for the toss with Rahul. The cheer was such that I wondered if we were playing at Eden Gardens or Chinnaswamy.

We were batting first and I duly registered the honour of playing the first delivery in the history of the IPL tournament sent down by Zaheer Khan. I was partnering Brendon McCullum, who single-handedly destroyed RCB.

It seemed the RCB bowlers had not adapted to T20 cricket.

We had an opening partnership of 61, where I just contributed 10. My job remained restricted to watching Brendon from the non-striker's end. He was magnificent and went on to score an unbeaten 158 off 73 balls. I watched Brendon closely as he had experience of playing T20 cricket in New Zealand. For me, his innings was an absolute eye-opener. It taught all of us what it takes to succeed in this form of cricket. Fast hands, quick reflexes, power and superb hand–eye coordination.

We scored 222 and the momentum was such that the winner almost got decided when our innings ended. RCB was under tremendous pressure from ball one and folded up for 82. We had a huge win and Shah Rukh, who was present for the first match, seemed elated.

We were to attend a post-match dinner at the UB House, hosted by Vijay Mallya. We arrived at the scheduled time but there was no sign of RCB. We couldn't see Mallya either. He arrived a little later and seemed very upset by the loss. RCB players were spotted after nearly an hour and their mood too was very sombre.

I told myself that this was new territory. The big franchise world was not cricket as we knew it. Here the rules were clearly different. Here the owners did not have the patience to hand-hold players during losses. They couldn't stand failure and wanted overnight results. They had a completely different mindset.

I would say in KKR we were perhaps in a marginally better situation as Shah Rukh being a top film star, who worked in a creative industry of hits and flops, understood athletes a shade better. We won our second match as well and all seemed well. The media started saying KKR was on a roll.

But our happiness ended the minute McCullum and three other players left for their New Zealand duties. Ricky Ponting had to leave as well and with their departures our fortunes nosedived. The early wins had inspired our fans. Now we started to disappoint them.

To make matters worse, replacement players were not up to the mark. I was the captain of the team but I had no idea that the replacement list had already been finalized. I was just informed at the team meeting that a couple of players were being brought in as replacements – Salman Butt, Mohammad Hafeez, Tatenda Taibu, etc.

I was both surprised and confused. Strictly from a cricketing point of view, better players ought to have been picked. Because of those wrong choices the team was left with only two match-winning, dependable batsmen in David Hussey and myself. We won a few games after that – I got a 57 ball 91 in Hyderabad against Deccan Chargers – but didn't win enough to qualify for the knock-out.

I had insisted that the coach and the team owner pick Shoaib Akhtar at the auction. They had pointed out his inconsistent history. But I was pretty sure that I would be able to handle him. After all I was quite used to handling players effectively during my tenure as the Indian captain.

I knew Shoaib's blistering pace was bound to make a difference in the shortest format. In fact it did. We knocked out Sehwag's belligerent Delhi splendidly as the Rawalpindi Express cleaned them up, and Eden roared in delight. Shoaib took 4 wickets for 11 runs and we won a low-scoring match. It was one of our most memorable wins but we could not sustain it.

Handling Shoaib turned out to be more difficult than I had imagined. Instead of turning around the competition for us, Shoaib suddenly decided not to play any more. He withdrew after making only three appearances despite my repeated requests.

He said he had an injury, but I for one found his injury mysterious. I pleaded with him that he had to send down only four overs. I said even with a small, niggling injury he must play. But it was impossible to get him on the park.

Our batting depth was already affected and now with Shoaib's exit KKR's fortunes plummeted further. I was looking at his IPL stats the other day. The three matches that Shoaib played for KKR produced five wickets with a mind-blowing average. But if such a bowler suddenly decides to go away, the team gets severely affected.

By the time we came back for season two, I had already announced my retirement from first-class cricket. There were a number of problems in holding the IPL in India including the general elections and it went to South Africa. I remember players assembling in Kolkata in March. Our coach John Buchanan was already there. He called me for a meeting one day at the iconic Oberoi Grand. This was where I first got a hint that I might be losing my captaincy.

I did not know whether the owners had any idea about this but they had entrusted the entire responsibility to the coach who had clearly made up his mind. In running a national team it was unthinkable that a coach would decide the captain's fate. Even someone as powerful as Chappell needed the approval of the selectors. Again, IPL was different.

I was taken aback by John's decision. When I asked John who he was appointing as captain, the answer came as a bit of a shock. He said there would be four different captains. I have never heard such a thing in cricket. John kept on saying all the captains would have a fair role. I just looked at him in stunned silence.

It was utterly confusing for me. In all these years of observing and playing cricket I had known the captain to be the most important player in winning battles. Here this man was saying its complete opposite.

I was told by one of the overseas players that John believed cricket should go the football way, where a manager was the supremo, where he had all the powers and dictated the captain. I begged to disagree but that meant very little to anyone.

Anyway, we arrived in South Africa and headed to Bloemfontein where a training camp had been organized. Why Bloemfontein of all places? Because the fitness trainer lived there. But I must say the camp was organized well. It was also our first taste of John's multiple captaincy model.

Eventually Brendon McCullum was appointed the official skipper for the season. But he was not alone and could only captain through a partnership with three other gentlemen. The three other captains for off-the-field captaincy were Matthew Mort, Andy Bichel and John himself.

They would sit in three different parts of the stadium. One behind the sight screen. One went to point. The third sat near the pavilion. They had four walkie-talkies and constantly shared inputs among themselves. The on-field captain, McCullum, had to look at one of them and take directions for running the team.

I was shocked. I had not understood the operations but was very keen on understanding them. I wanted to see how McCullum would use this flow of information. Mind you, on the field, apart from him, there were two other 'administrative' captains in Brad Hodge and the wicketkeeper. In this format the keeper was very important as he set the field and sent hand signals to the bowlers.

I was standing at mid-off and following McCullum. For the first time in my life I saw a captain look over the sight screen to receive signals and then look towards Brad Hodge to get instructions. We had different signals for different deliveries.

It was also the first time I saw a bowler looking for instructions before sending down each delivery. Ashok Dinda, our pace bowling spearhead, would go back to the top of his bowling mark, wait for a fraction of a second to get a signal and only then start his run. I found this almost unbelievable.

That night I went out for dinner with fellow KKR player Chris Gayle. Gayle too was as worried and confused as I was. What is going on, he asked me. I expressed helplessness and said I truly didn't know. What you see is what is going on. Gayle laughed out loud in his characteristic fashion and said, 'Then I think we are headed for disaster.'

I felt sorry for Brendon. Such an outstanding T20 cricketer became a victim in this chaos. He didn't even decide the batting order. During one match he had won the toss and I asked him, what number are you and me going at? Are we opening? He answered, 'I don't know.' He had to wait for John to give him the batting order.

Not surprisingly, our performance in the tournament was awful. I performed badly as my mind was all messed up. I have always believed that players are made or destroyed by leadership. KKR's performance in the second season was the worst in its IPL history.

As we kept losing matches, panic set in among the team members. The supply line was very poor as we did not have a solid reserve bench. IPL was different from the national team in so many ways. Here the auction was all important. You could even afford to lose a few matches but a bad auction meant you were hobbled for three successive years. The damage was much bigger.

Confidence is the most important cologne that you can have in a cricket dressing room. We were inducted into a new world of cricket. Not even one player in that team including Brendon had clarity of what was happening.

So one night I told Brendon, listen, it is slipping away. We have to do something as a team. But we couldn't reverse the downslide as by then the asking rate for staging a reverse in the tournament had climbed too high.

John was sacked following our disastrous performance. He was not even asked to come back to India and submit his report to the management. He grumbled and said a few unpalatable things in the media, but who was going to listen to that? He was in charge and the team had failed completely.

Buchanan saga over, we now moved on to season three. A new coach was picked – Dav Whatmore. Once again I was brought back as the captain. I told myself, look at the extremes:

First year: Captain

Second year: Just an ordinary member

Third year: Captain

As always, I failed to understand how I could be so bad and so good within a period of only twelve months. But then in franchise cricket you only do as you are told.

Our fortunes did not change much in season three. As I said earlier, once you picked a team at the auction you had to stick with it for three years. The damage thus lingered on. My own performance in season three was the best. The team also performed better than it had in the previous two seasons. But we weren't good enough to qualify.

I knew the team was now up for a change and rightly so as the previous unit had not delivered. Our performance was below par and KKR needed a shaking up. With fresh auctions coming up the management needed to acquire the right kind of players and not repeat the mistakes that were made earlier.

I was all for it. But I did not realize that I would not

even be retained as a player. Personally I had a great year notwithstanding the dismal team performance. I was the highest scorer for my team having scored 493 runs with an average of 37.58. The strike rate was 117. Sachin had won the Orange Cap with 618 runs and I was fourth in the overall run-getters list. The numbers spoke for themselves, but yet again they were overlooked.

In a country versus country test format, so many players have struggled initially. Their captains or selectors have hand-held those talents during the period. Have kept faith in them. How many names do you want? Steve Waugh, Jacques Kallis, Dilip Vengsarkar, the list is endless.

I have always endorsed a leadership point of view that once you are convinced about someone's class you allow him to blossom despite a few failures. But you need patience. During my years as the Indian captain I have hand-held a few players as well. We were patient. As I said, this was a different world. Different ground rules.

I had requested Venky to allow me some days to think. Finally I got back to him saying that as an athlete I knew that my time would be up sooner or later. But I still saw some batting years left in me. So mentoring was not an option that I would consider at this stage. Venky did not seem very convinced. I realized from his body language that they would go in at the auction without me in their plans.

Coming back to Shah Rukh, I had interacted a lot with him during my time with KKR. By the third season his involvement was even deeper. The team's series of poor performances had hurt him deeply. I could understand his plight too. Being such a super successful performer it was difficult to take repeated failures in a product that bore his signature.

I used to be in constant touch with him and in season three more than once took his opinion while deciding upon the final eleven – something I had never done while picking an Indian eleven. But as I said, the IPL was managed and played in a completely different way.

I was later asked by the media what would have happened if the same KKR team had been owned by any other superstar? I replied that non-performance was an issue no one would have tolerated. So I thought the decision to leave me out from captaincy was quite justified. But how could they leave me out from the side as a batsman? To me, that was unjustified.

I was also asked many times if someone had poisoned Shah Rukh's ears against me. My answer has been the same, I don't think so. There was a theory doing the rounds that my chest-thumping in a particular match against Deccan Chargers at Eden Gardens had angered the KKR management.

Now to give you the background. I usually do not watch TV or read the paper on the day of the match. But that day before leaving for the ground, I had switched on the TV. What I saw was a banner headline, 'Time for Ganguly to Retire'. Some said it was part of an organized campaign. Some media friends felt it was politically designed. I still don't know who the mastermind was.

That day I scored 88 runs and we won the match against Deccan Chargers. I was full of raw emotion – the anger of the afternoon news still simmered in me. That's what led to my actions. Performers at times react like this when they are unnecessarily brought under the scanner. Someone as cool and dignified as Dravid reacted once he got past his hundred in that historic Kolkata Test match in 2001. There are many such incidents in the world of sports.

You have to understand the sentiment of the performers. They get scrutinized almost constantly. The spotlight is often too much, sometimes an emotional explosion is understandable. My reaction that day was directed towards whoever had put up the banner. It came from passion and love for the game. The high of success, nothing more. Remember how Federer reacted on court after winning a Grand Slam or Maradona at a World Cup. It certaintly was not directed at Shah Rukh or any other members of the management.

Eventually KKR's decision not to retain me did not come in the way of my personal friendship with Shah Rukh. They were well within their rights to do so. When we met subsequently we were as normal as ever.

My last IPL season saw me playing for Pune. We had a match against KKR at Eden Gardens. It was 5 May. Of course it attracted unprecedented interest in Kolkata. After the match Shah Rukh came to our dressing room and suggested that we go for a walk around the stadium and thank the crowd. He would always do that when we worked together. I readily said yes. We had just lost a close match and I was understandably upset. But Shah Rukh was kind. He said, 'Dada, I can see they really love you in Kolkata.'

17

The Final Pune Exit

I was taking guard at the Rajiv Gandhi International Stadium in Hyderabad when I saw the ball being handed over to the fastest bowler on the planet. As they say in Bond movies, the name's Dale. Dale Steyn.

For a minute I found the setting completely unreal. Here I was staging a comeback in the IPL after being left out in the auction. I had almost no practice. Almost zero preparation. And in a one-ball sport, I had to battle the fastest bowler. That's the magic of sport at the top level. No freebies, as they say.

In my life there has been no absence of dramas. No absence of controversies. A fresh one had erupted in the media after my non-inclusion at the Bengaluru auction. This was the auction for IPL season four. With KKR turning their back on me, I had to move on to some other franchise.

There were a few phone calls and enquiries before the auction. I wasn't sure which team would pick me – life hardly follows a script that you have prepared. Next morning, while watching the auction at my place I discovered much to my dismay that no one picked me.

By then I had got dropped a few times. So I wasn't shocked. But it was terribly disappointing. The next day there was another auction for the leftover players. I knew I wouldn't get picked this time either. I was right.

I realized I had very little chance of playing the IPL in the future as I wasn't getting any younger. What was the point in pursuing domestic cricket then in front of half-empty galleries? I decided to end my career with Bengal.

Dear reader, you must understand that in life nothing is guaranteed. You will never know what awaits you at the next crossing. When faced with rejection at work, our first reaction is invariably disappointment.

But if there's anything you should take away from this book, it is that you should not give up. Be patient. You have to wait for your turn, and when it comes, you must remain prepared.

In the case of an athlete, he mustn't stop training. When an opportunity resurfaces, he should be able to stand up and deliver. There is no room for self-pity. And you have to also keep in mind that what you did yesterday has no meaning. History has no takers. Everything is about today and tomorrow.

This time though I didn't want to fight. The only consolation was that some of the greats of my generation were going through the same predicament. The Dravids and the Pontings who'd had such outstanding records at the international level were also suffering the franchise onslaught.

Midway through the tournament I received a call from Saharashri Subrata Roy. He was the owner of the new entrant Pune Warriors. Their bowler Ashish Nehra had got injured. Saharashri said, please come and join my team. I was completely unprepared for this turn of events. As I hung up the phone, all I could think of were my bats! I didn't have enough. I sent an urgent message to my bat manufacturer in Meerut saying I needed three immediately.

Our next match was in Hyderabad against Deccan Chargers. When I landed in Hyderabad I was pretty nervous. I was a bit scared that without any practice I might make a fool of myself. I spent the flight from Kolkata to Hyderabad reassuring myself that if I had done it once I could do it again. I played back past performances in my head to instil courage and confidence in myself.

I landed in Hyderabad and hit the nets for the next two days. I felt like a beginner who was learning how to bat. I was hardly in the right physical shape and tried my best to make up for it mentally. I kept visualizing my past performances. It was a nerve-racking situation. I knew the entire country would be watching me play.

The first few seconds before I faced up to Steyn were crucial. I concentrated my entire energy on the twenty-two yards. I was pushing myself to get right behind those express deliveries. I charged myself up by imagining I was a heavyweight boxer who was lying flat on the ground badly beaten up. But the moment the referee started counting, I got up to deliver the knockout punch.

It was a test of my experience and resolve. Well, as luck would have it the first delivery hit the middle of the bat. The sound of the ball hitting the middle of the bat transformed me completely. I became the Sourav Ganguly of old, the player who for fifteen years believed every day that he was good enough to score runs for India. I remained not out on 32 and won the low-target match for Pune.

When I was hitting Dale Steyn and Ishant Sharma repeatedly over the covers, a fan jumped on to the ground over an 8-foot fencing, evaded the security and fell at my feet. He told me I was one of the best cricketers he had ever seen. The security was soon all over him but I requested them to ease off and not take any action. I was very touched by his daring and passion.

After the match I sat all by myself. I was a satisfied and relieved man having made a mini comeback in the international arena. What made me immensely happy was that I was back on a cricket field and that I had not made a fool of myself despite being so underprepared. I had loved that cricket pitch forever.

I went up to our captain, Yuvraj Singh. It was such an amazing reversal of roles. Here was the young boy who made his debut under me. Someone I had hand-held. Today the same person had thrown in his unconditional support. He had kept faith in my ability. Could it get more satisfying?

The season duly ran its course and Pune didn't qualify. They had won 60 per cent of their matches after my arrival. But the initial losses were far too many to handle. On my part I ended the season on a happy note believing that I would get one more season of the IPL.

My second season with Pune was nearing and I was extra determined to peform well. I did not spare any effort and worked as if I was eyeing an India cap. I went through the full grind of domestic cricket, scored lots of runs in domestic cricket and at the request of Mr Dalmiya even agreed to lead Bengal. We ended up winning the Vijay Hazare Trophy in Delhi.

In January I got a call from Saharashri Subrata Roy to come and meet him in Delhi. I went on a Sunday. He got to the point rather quickly: 'Sourav, I have decided, you will be our captain this season.'

I was in a bind. A thought crossed my mind that I was replacing Yuvraj, someone who had provided shelter to me just a few months ago. I didn't know how to respond. I only wondered what to tell Yuvi. Would he think, I helped this man so much and now he has plotted my dismissal?

I requested Saharashri not to make the news public and wait for a couple of days. I left the meeting thinking here was another victim of the ruthless franchise mindset. One season of bad performance and the Man of the Tournament in the 2011 World Cup bites the dust. I have not seen international captains lose their job in eight weeks. But in the IPL too many captains have been replaced in less than a month's time.

My relation with Yuvi has always been rock solid from the time I knew him. I went out of the room and called him immediately. I told him what had been communicated to me. To my surprise he said he knew of it. I told him that I had not planned for this to happen and if he wanted I would not accept the position and carry on as a player. Thankfully, Yuvi believed everything that I told him.

As I boarded the Delhi–Kolkata flight my mind was all mixed up. I was thinking, how can I be so good and so bad in such a short time? Just seven months ago I had got rejected at the auction and today I am being asked to lead an IPL team? There was no answer to this riddle.

I decided to concentrate on the areas which I could somewhat control. The priority had to be the auction. The IPL auction room was the place where winners got separated from the rest. It was the auction, and the proper team selection, that decided if you would win or lose.

I was preparing desperately to get a strong team. I also consulted the owners since their decision was final and binding. In the franchise format the owners needed to be informed of every small thing. It is much more important than the captain's individual choice. This was quite different from the way I had led India. But then in the rush, rush superfast lane of the IPL, history is meant only for the history books.

Having done extensive homework, I landed for the auction in Bengaluru. I had arrived a day before to have an important meeting with the management. I sat with Abhijit Sarkar, who has always been a very important person in the Sahara set-up. I have always shared a wonderful rapport with Abhijitda. He was with us even during the South Africa World Cup when Sahara was our team sponsor. We had a detailed discussion that night, which coach Allan Donald also joined. We made all the preparations and retired to our respective rooms.

Next morning I woke up early and had breakfast. As I was getting ready to go down, my doorbell rang. I opened the door and found a pensive-looking Abhijitda standing outside. He said, 'A decision has come from the Boss that we will not participate in the auction.'

I got the shock of my life! What was he saying? I desperately tried to make him understand the impact of such a decision. How irreparable the damage would be. The Boss's anger with the board may subside afterwards. But we would not get another opportunity to pick the players we wanted. I begged and pleaded.

Finally, Abhijitda called the Boss and handed over the mobile to me. I pleaded again but found him very adamant. He said his decision was final and that we needed to get out of Bengaluru as soon as possible. He was the owner. He was the boss. You could hardly argue. You could only obey.

We left the city and were put on different flights by the management. I was pretty downcast. I would be leader of a group which I had neither selected nor would be able to strengthen. I knew for a team that had played so badly last season, missing the auction was suicidal. I knew even before the first ball was bowled that we were done and dusted.

We then went to the leftovers from the auction to reinforce the team. The current Australian captain, Steve Smith, who was largely unknown then, got picked. Michael Clarke also remained unsold and I was asked to consider him. I didn't know how he would fare and solve our problems. But I was asked to take him and I did.

We began in spectacular fashion despite missing an out-of-sorts Yuvraj for the entire season. We won in Mumbai against the formidable Mumbai Indians. After the match, rival captain Bhajji said at the press conference that my captaincy had made all the difference in this match. It was of course pleasing to the ears but I knew the momentum would be difficult to handle with this team. After six matches we were the number one team in the tournament and managed to beat the mighty Chennai Super Kings in Pune.

The team members were in a super excited state of mind when we went to Bengaluru to play RCB. Batting first we had put up a big total and had them under control. When Ashish Nehra came to bowl the last over, RCB needed 24 runs for a victory. Nehra has been one of the best death bowlers and it was unthinkable that he would concede so many in the last over. De Villiers has to be given credit as well. He played some unbelievable strokes and turned the game.

I had never imagined we would lose this match. We started declining from this point on. I think along the way we lost momentum. Worse, panic set in and with it confusion. I was asked to drop Nehra from the playing eleven. But I resisted. I tried to reason that the very nature of T20 cricket was such you will have six good games and one terrible one. But the bosses were impatient, unrelenting. They simply didn't want to listen.

They wanted to effect changes in the batting order as well. Disappointed, I led the team at Kotla against the power-packed batting unit of Delhi Daredevils. In my hotel room that night I quietly celebrated the win, which I thought would change the momentum again in our favour. I scored 41, took two wickets and walked away with the Player of the Match title. Not bad for a thirty-nine-year-old who was considered not good enough at the auction just a season ago.

We eventually came down to Kolkata to play the biggest match of the season against KKR. As I landed in Kolkata the first thing I was told was that the demand for tickets had reached an all-time high. As soon as I landed, I saw that this was easily going to be the biggest match of the season.

The media had added their own angle to the match, hyping it as Dada versus SRK. All kinds of gossip and rumours were flying about, and a mad frenzy was building around the match. I quickly went back to my old routine – removing myself completely from the madness and creating my own little zone of solitude. I knew I had to treat each ball on its own merit and not get influenced by the situation. I even switched off my cell phone in the evening before the match. I had never done this before in my entire cricketing career.

On the day of the match I entered the team meeting to announce the eleven. Immediately afterwards I was told that the bosses were looking for me. It was Mr Roy on the phone who wanted to know about the combination that I was playing. He wanted to make certain changes and naturally I had to follow his order.

I wanted to open in this match and take control right from the word go but was advised against it. I was told instead that I had to bat lower down the order. The boss's idea was that if we were chasing I could control the middle order with my experience and win the game for Pune.

I had played at Eden Gardens at different stages of my life. But I have rarely seen the kind of hysteria that was on display. On one side of the stadium they had the KKR flags. On the other the Blue Pune flags. From a distance, I could see a few banners that said 'Dada versus Kolkata'.

The atmosphere was so nerve-racking that some of our

relatively inexperienced players had a problem adjusting. KKR started off at a blistering pace and only towards the end of their innings could we control them. They scored 150, which I thought was highly gettable.

But while chasing we were in deep trouble. Five wickets fell when we were just 50-plus. It was left to Angelo Mathews and myself to pull our team out of the crisis and try for a win. We had a big partnership and got close to the target. Angelo scored 35. I got 36. But we lost by seven runs. Thereafter we collapsed. This was exactly what I had feared – quality players would have handled the pressure much better.

The game was my last hope in the tournament. From this defeat, we just went down and down. Ironically, the last match of my international career had KKR as the opponents. We lost this match in Pune and the season ended for us.

I told myself that I would not play IPL any more. I spent nearly a month thinking about it but the voice within told me that my time was up. I had felt the same when I decided to retire from Test cricket. After a month or so I informed my family.

I was due to see Saharashri soon as I'd been invited to his granddaughter's rice ceremony in Mumbai. I attended the function and told him that I thought the team now needed to move on and find a new captain for the next season. And with that conversation, I brought an end to my sixteen-year international cricketing career. In July I would be forty.

Through my cricket I had seen an entire cycle of life. Right from my debut in Brisbane to the last day in Pune, it had been an amazing journey. A journey that had seen everything. From despair to ecstasy. From super success to a first-ball duck. From tremendous match-winning performances to disappointing ones. My memories of the last IPL season were very precious. The hysteria at Hyderabad, the passion at Kolkata, the action-packed last over in Bengaluru. It was a good way to go.

My two decades in cricket taught me several important lessons. I have already shared some of them with you. I would like to share a few more here.

In your life you may come across people who will harm you. For no fault of yours they become your enemies and damage your growth. What do you do with them? A lot of us (at one point of time I was no exception) think of settling the score.

Today as a happily retired middle-aged cricketer I would advise you not to resort to revenge. There is no point dwelling on people who are not worthy of your attention. You will only be expending negative energy and more importantly wasting precious time. They don't deserve that.

I would urge all young professionals to channel that energy into their own well-being. Be the best that you can be. For years I lived knowing that one ball would decide the course of my life. Just ignore your detractors and be so good at your work that they fall by the wayside. Bettering your performance is the best solution for a professional. The rest doesn't matter. Trust me, it is very tasty.

Another obstacle that quite often puts a barrier on performance is constant criticism. The thick-skinned ones absorb it well but the sensitive one gets deeply affected.

Cricket is such a mind game that if you get even slightly affected, you will be unable to play fearlessly. So if you are looking for a high-quality performance you will have to learn to quickly send unwanted criticism to spam.

You will be criticized for what you do in a keenly followed profession. From my entry into the international arena to the last day I went out as the Pune Warriors captain I was analysed. But even as a twenty-three-year-old, I did not allow it to dampen my spirits. My take on this is simple. Criticism is part and parcel of professional life. If you do not get criticized in your profession it will mean that your profession is not important enough. In any aspect of life if you get accolades be also prepared for the brickbats, which come with the package. I always knew it and did not lose any sleep over it.

Pressure is another key thing to master. It will be with you as long as you continue to attempt breaking barriers, set targets or retain your reputation. In my career there were moments when the pressure seemed unbearable. Yet I never ran away from it. The rule of the professional jungle suggests that to win battles you have to embrace pressure and not get frightened.

A good two to three years into retirement, I was playing a veterans' series organized by Tendulkar and Warne in America. All the top stars were playing and I didn't get runs in the first match. This was not surprising as my stint with the Cricket Association of Bengal allowed me virtually no time for practising.

I could have easily avoided taking any pressure for the second match of the series in Los Angeles as it would not have added to my tally of international scores. Nor would anyone have remembered. But I decided to push myself as I had during my playing days, took the additional pressure and got runs in the second.

As I said, it did not change anything. Not a single run was added to my tally. But deep inside there was enormous satisfaction of having handled pressure successfully yet again. I tell you, pressure is like a wild horse. Difficult to tame but once you manage to do it the skill set remains with you.

For a lot of players handling retirement has not been easy. I have, however, thought positive all along. When I did a stocktaking it did not look unimpressive. In that generation of Indian players I was the fastest to reach 9000 runs in one-day cricket. Only the third player in the world to score 10,000 runs and take 100 wickets. Captain of 200 games for India. One of the top special three in Indian cricket to have played 100 Tests and 300 one-dayers. I could leave with my head held very high.

Of course I would be parting from the thing I loved the most. We cricketers lived a full, action-packed life. In the last two decades, I had experienced so much. Rejections, my debut hundred, being ousted, taken back as captain, not picked at the auction, again picked as captain.

I come from a very conservative Bengali family with little exposure to life. But cricket taught me about life in all its shades and colours. Sitting in that Pune hotel room, busy packing my bags, I told myself, there was a bigger part of life still to be lived. And enjoyed. Even the greatest of athletes had to embrace retirement. Sampras, Lara,

Tendulkar, Maradona. The best part was that we left the sport when we were relatively young. The path ahead was wide open for us.

Only cricket has finished. Life was calling me for a much longer and more challenging second innings. Umpire, middle stump, please.

Acknowledgements

My thanks to my co-writer Gautam Bhattacharya, who was so committed to writing this, to my manager Partho for making it all possible and to Chiki Sarkar and the entire Juggernaut team who worked so tirelessly to bring this book out.

Photograph Credits

p. 1, top: author's personal collection; bottom: Suman Chattopadhyay

p. 2, top: Getty Images; bottom: Joy Sengupta

p. 3, top and bottom: Suman Chattopadhyay

p. 4, top and bottom: Suman Chattopadhyay

p. 5, top: Getty Images; bottom: Suman Chattopadhyay

p. 6, top and bottom: Suman Chattopadhyay

p. 7: Suman Chattopadhyay

p. 8, top: Getty Images; bottom: Suman Chattopadhyay

p. 9, top and bottom: Suman Chattopadhyay

p. 10, top and bottom: Suman Chattopadhyay

p. 11, top: Getty Images; bottom: Suman Chattopadhyay

p. 12, top and bottom: Suman Chattopadhyay

Photograph Credits

p. 13, top and bottom left and right: Suman Chattopadhyay

p. 14, top and bottom: Suman Chattopadhyay

p. 15, top and bottom: Suman Chattopadhyay

p. 16, top right and bottom: Joy Sengupta

THE APP
FOR INDIAN
READERS

Fresh, original books tailored for mobile and for India. Starting at ₹10.

www.juggernaut.in

CRAFTED
FOR MOBILE
READING

*Thought you would never read a book
on mobile? Let us prove you wrong.*

www.juggernaut.in

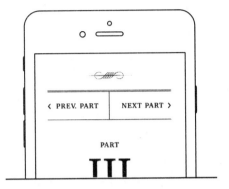

Beautiful Typography

The quality of print transferred
to your mobile. Forget ugly PDFs.

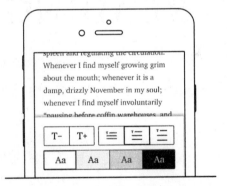

Customizable Reading

Read in the font size, spacing
and background of your liking.

AN EXTENSIVE LIBRARY

Fresh new original Juggernaut books from the likes of Sunny Leone, Twinkle Khanna, Rujuta Diwekar, William Dalrymple, Pankaj Mishra, Arundhati Roy and lots more. Plus, books from partner publishers and all the free classics you want.

DON'T JUST READ; INTERACT

We're changing the reading experience from passive to active.

www.juggernaut.in

Ask authors questions

Get all your answers from the horse's mouth.
Juggernaut authors actually reply to every
question they can.

Rate and review

Let everyone know of your favourite reads or
critique the finer points of a book – you will be
heard in a community of like-minded readers.

Gift books to friends

For a book-lover, there's no nicer gift than
a book personally picked. You can even
do it anonymously if you like.

Enjoy new book formats

Discover serials released in parts over
time, picture books including comics,
and story-bundles at discounted rates.

www.juggernaut.in

4

LOWEST PRICES & ONE-TAP BUYING

Books start at ₹10 with regular discounts and free previews.

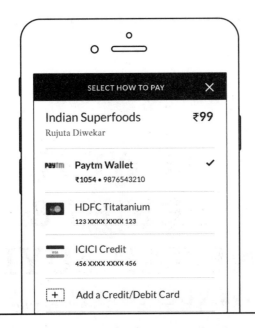

Paytm Wallet, Cards & Apple Payments

On Android, just add a Paytm Wallet once and buy any book with one tap. On iOS, pay with one tap with your iTunes-linked debit/credit card.

Click the QR Code with a QR scanner app
or type the link into the Internet browser
on your phone to download the app.

SCAN TO READ THIS
BOOK ON YOUR PHONE

www.juggernaut.in

DOWNLOAD THE APP

www.juggernaut.in

For our complete catalogue, visit www.juggernaut.in
To submit your book, send a synopsis and two
sample chapters to books@juggernaut.in
For all other queries, write to contact@juggernaut.in